A.M.

...think it would be
...to have the
...drill drinks on
...ch outside the
...g-room
...also that you
...nice Boy.

...though I know
...above it is
...in a
But it's the only thing
...get through
...misses you
...it told
...fully — It's
...a satisfactory
day, only
I had with
...last evening don't make the
...goodness ...out alas —
...bless WE my
sweetheart.
David

Mrs Simpson
Hotel Meurice
Paris
France

THE FORT,
SUNNINGDALE, ASCOT.

WE have him to
look after our
interests — As soon
about Walter ...
being transferred

H.M. The King

...the morning
...finish ...
...send by air mail
...so as you can read
...all I have to say as
...quickly as possible
...God bless WE

Be calm with B —
But tell the country
To-morrow I am lost —
...you but Perry and
Myself can discreetly
Manage or will let Baldwin
know —
A big big ...

...decided
...a walking
...an occasional
...scandal
...about WE
...a spy that
...by people
...the project this
...I must remain

The Duchess of Windsor

The DUCHESS of WINDSOR

Michael Bloch

*

Weidenfeld & Nicolson
London

First published in Great Britain in 1996 by
George Weidenfeld & Nicolson Ltd

Weidenfeld & Nicolson Ltd
The Orion Publishing Group
Orion House
5 Upper St Martin's Lane
London WC2H 9EA

A catalogue record for this book is available from the British Library.

ISBN 0297 83590 4

Book design by Ronald Clark
Printed in Italy

TO ANDREW ROBERTS

remembering 9 King's Parade

Contents

Preface

1996 is an apt year to remember the Duchess of Windsor. It will be ten years since her death on 24 April, and a hundred years since her birth on 19 June. 20 January commemorates the sixtieth anniversary of Edward VIII's accession to the British throne, which he dreamt of sharing with her, while 11 December will mark sixty years since he gave up that throne, against her wishes, in order to marry her.

Moreover, it seems possible that the Prince and Princess of Wales will divorce in 1996. Things have indeed come full circle since 1936, when the main objection to King Edward's marrying the woman he loved lay in the fact of her having been the innocent party in two divorce cases. It is hard to remember that, fifty years ago, no divorced person could hold senior office under the crown; forty years ago, Princess Margaret was unable to marry Peter Townsend largely because he had been divorced; and little more than twenty years ago, Lord Harewood was not allowed to attend the funeral of his uncle the Duke of Windsor (of whom he had been fond) as he had divorced and remarried some years earlier. Since then, the Queen's sister has divorced; her daughter has divorced and remarried; and her two elder sons, having wedded daughters of divorced parents, now seem set to put an end to their marriages. Fortunately for all concerned, their divorce proceedings are unlikely to involve any formal enquiries into questions of marital fidelity, as would probably have been the case sixty years ago.

During their marriage, the Windsors (and especially the Duchess) were widely regarded as leading a somewhat disreputable life; but as one surveys the current scene, how respectable they seem! They were happily and faithfully married for thirty-five years, throughout which time he remained deeply in love with her, and she devoted herself to his comfort and well-being. Long before the British tabloids got to work on the Royal Family, the Duke and Duchess were viciously attacked in the American popular press for almost everything they did or did not do; but they withstood this criticism bravely and it never affected their marriage. And how innocent now appear the things for which they were criticized – the globe-trotting, the association with film stars and other celebrities, the efforts (not unsuccessful) to keep up a royal style on a limited income. They had some reason for regarding the British Establishment as 'the enemy', but never lost their sense of humour, and when interviewed on BBC television in 1970, virtually confined themselves to discussing their domestic happiness.

This book does not aim to be a comprehensive biography of the Duchess, but I have tried to capture something of her personality, explain the main episodes of her much-misunderstood life, and to touch on certain aspects which may lead to a better knowledge of her. I have not burdened it with source notes, but have drawn on the Windsor correspondence which I published in the 1980s, and have mentioned in the short bibliography the other works from which I have quoted or to which I have referred.

I am grateful to the many people who helped me when I was writing about the Windsors in the 1980s, and particularly to the late Maître Suzanne Blum, a much-missed friend. More recent debts which I gratefully acknowledge are to Leo Abse, Ariane Bankes, Andrew and Jackie Best, Stephen Carroll, Ronald Clark, Graham Crowden, Jean-Pierre Dagorne, Jason Davies, Michael Dover, Susie Dowdall, Robert Elliott, Jonathan Fryer, Ronald Irving, James Lees-Milne, Robbie and Glyn Macdonald, Professor R.B. McDowell, Gordon McKenzie, Annette Rémond, Peter Robinson, Royce and Morar Ryton, Anne Seagrim, Florian Stahmer, Chris Townsend, Moray Watson, Wynyard Wilkinson and Antony Wood; to Jane Mays of the *Daily Mail* and Alexandra Rhodes of Sotheby's, for making available photographs reproduced herein; to Edith Stokes and all at Mount Pleasant; to the manager and staff of the Savoy Hotel, Madeira; and to my parents.

Michael Bloch
20 January 1996

I have always had the courage for the new things that life sometimes offers. . . .

Wallis Simpson to her Aunt Bessie, 4 May 1936

*

I should . . . be tempted to classify her as An American Woman par excellence, but for the suspicion that she is not a woman at all. . . .

James Pope-Hennessy on the Duchess of Windsor, January 1958

An indeterminate-looking Wallis, a few months old, in the arms of her mother,
Alice Montague Warfield.

CHAPTER ONE

'I can't go on wandering'

The future Duchess of Windsor was born at Blue Ridge Summit, Pennsylvania, on 19 June 1896. She was called Wallis after her father, Teackle Wallis Warfield, who in turn had been named after Severn Teackle Wallis, a prominent Maryland lawyer-politician who had been a friend of the family.

A fact which has puzzled biographers and historians is that her birth was not registered, nor was it announced in the newspapers of Baltimore, where the families of both her parents were prominent. The explanation normally given is that her parents had been married only eight months, and were anxious, in a society obsessed with correct behaviour, not to draw attention to the possibility that their child might have been conceived out of wedlock. Yet the birth was premature, as the doctor long afterwards testified. In the light of her masculine adult appearance, another possible explanation suggests itself. Might not the future Duchess, at the outset of her existence, have exhibited some signs of gender confusion? If such were the case, it would certainly account for her parents' reluctance to proclaim the baby's arrival, either officially or socially, as well as their decision to confer on it a name giving few clues as to its sex. (She was eventually baptized Bessie Wallis, but 'Bessie' was never used by anyone except her grandmother.)

Her pedigree was aristocratic by American standards. The Warfields had long been prominent in the political and business life of Maryland, while her mother, Alice Montague, hailed from an old Virginia line: each family produced a governor of its respective state. Yet the two families, though both staunchly 'Southern', and closely identified with the Confederate cause during the Civil War, were very different in character. The Warfields were a stern, hardworking Protestant dynasty, who had prospered during the nineteenth century; the Montagues, once important landowners, were now impoverished gentry trading on their wit, *joie de vivre* and good looks. The Duchess believed that, through her parents, she had inherited two conflicting strains – the Warfield toughness and practical ability, the Montague gentleness and artistic sensibility. Thus, within her, the ambitious mingled with the easygoing, the respectable with the Bohemian, the serious with the lighthearted, the chaste with the sensual, the calculating with the spontaneous, the masculine with the feminine.

Her parents were a handsome young couple, and much in love. But her father suffered from tuberculosis; it was in search of a cure that he had gone to the Pennsylvanian mountains, where his daughter was unexpectedly born; and he died when she was only five months old. Left with little money, Alice and her baby went to live in Baltimore with her formidable Warfield mother-in-law. These two widows, her mother and paternal grandmother, were the main figures in Wallis's childhood, and presented a stark contrast. Alice was pretty and flirtatious, impractical and rather silly, but a gay, carefree, open spirit. In a life of adversity nothing seemed to daunt her. She was known for her laughter and her wisecracking wit. The Duchess later wrote that she had been more like an older sister than a mother. Her grandmother, on the other hand, was like a father. A stern, dominating, masculine figure, dressed in black weeds without jewellery or other ornament, she observed strict habits and standards, and ruled the world around her with a rod of iron. Amongst much else she instilled in her granddaughter a keen sense of economy and of the art of household man-agement.

The only man in the household was Wallis's bachelor uncle Solomon D. Warfield ('Uncle Sol'), a successful banker and President of the Continental Trust Company. He appears in her memoirs as a sinister and lecherous figure, of whom she was more than a little frightened; he was amorously interested in her mother, and may have directed his attentions towards Wallis herself during her infancy. (The memoirs hint at this.) At all events, it seems to have been on account of his behaviour that, when Wallis was about five, mother and daugh-ter suddenly moved out of the grandmaternal residence – though Uncle Sol continued to give them intermittent financial support, and Wallis continued to visit her grandmother most afternoons until she went to boarding school.

For a while Alice and Wallis lodged with Alice's elder sister, the kindly and forthright Bessie Merryman ('Aunt Bessie'), also a widow. After that, they lived in a succession of modest rented flats, sometimes taking in paying guests to make ends meet. Alice made sure that Wallis was always well-dressed, and sent her to the best local schools she could afford. Wallis later admitted that she had been spoiled by her mother, who too often allowed her to have her own way. She spent her holidays on the country estates of wealthy kinsfolk such as her uncle, Henry Warfield, at Timonium near Baltimore, or her mother's cousin, Lelia Montague Barnett, married to the general commanding the US Marine Corps, at Wakefield Manor in Virginia. Wallis must have been very conscious of her status as a poor relation, and this may have had an effect on her personality, filling her, later in life, with an intense desire for social and material success.

When Wallis was twelve, Alice remarried: her new husband was John Raisin, the indolent scion of a wealthy political family. Wallis was at first jealous of her stepfather (though the marriage seems to have had little sexual content, his nickname being 'the seedless raisin'). The family however now found itself in affluent circumstances, and Wallis was sent to Oldfields, a fashionable girls' boarding school in the Baltimore hills. 'Gentleness and courtesy are expected of girls at all times' was its motto; like all such establishments, it aimed to prepare its pupils for the marriage market. Wallis seems to have been happy there and to have made some close friends, including the pretty Mary Kirk. But when she was seventeen her stepfather died, and with him the private income that had sustained the family.

The fatherless Wallis was a romantic girl. During her holidays she became passionately attached to some of her older male cousins. Her inscription in the Oldfields school leaving book reads: 'All is love.' Her thoughts were concentrated on finding the man of her dreams. Unlike her mother, she was not delicately beautiful: in fact she had a decidedly masculine appearance, with an angular face, flat chest, and square hands and feet. In an effort to attract boys, she tended to play up this masculinity: she often dressed mannishly, parted her hair, and affected such mannerisms as wearing a monocle. She developed a somewhat bossy personality. Her male contemporaries found her different from other girls and many were attracted to her. Of course, such friendships were extremely innocent: girls in Wallis's position could never go out with a boy unless carefully chaperoned.

During the Baltimore social season of 1914–15, Alice, invoking the help of

Wallis (left) aged sixteen with Mary Kirk, her closest friend at Oldfields School: they were both eventually to marry Ernest Simpson.

rich relations, had Wallis brought out as a debutante: this was an essential preliminary to making a good match with a suitable *beau*. A few months later Wallis was invited to stay at Pensacola Naval Air Station in Florida, whose commandant was married to her mother's cousin Corrine, a celebrated beauty. Aviation was then in its infancy and a most hazardous and glamorous activity, and Wallis was quickly swept off her feet by one of the flying officers, E. Winfield Spencer Jr, with his devil-may-care personality and rugged looks. As a Northerner from a modest background and a mere junior grade lieutenant, he hardly represented the glittering match that her mother must have hoped for Wallis, who was eight years his junior. But Alice, who had herself married for

Wallis sporting a monocle, one of several boyish mannerisms she affected in girlhood.

Wallis as a Baltimore debutante during the Season of 1914–15.

love against the wishes of her family, did not oppose the marriage, which took place in November 1916.

The Duchess tells us in her memoirs that during their courtship 'Win' had been tender in his attentions towards her, but that all this changed on their wedding night, when she discovered that he was a heavy drinker. It would seem, however, that he also discovered something equally alarming about her. Twenty years later, before her marriage to the Duke of Windsor, Wallis is said to have confided to her friend Herman Rogers (who was to give her away to the Duke) that she had never had sexual intercourse with either of her previous husbands. If this is true it would follow that Spencer, after an engagement during which the proprieties had been observed, found that he was unable to possess his wife. As to whether this might have been due to some physiological defect on her part, or to some traumatic past incident in her life which had induced the condition known as *vaginismus*, or to some other cause, one can but speculate. But Spencer's dismay at his wife's incapacity may explain his indifference and cruelty towards her.

During the five years of their marriage, his drinking became progressively more serious and his behaviour towards her increasingly violent. He would beat her in his cups, and subject her to bizarre rituals such as forcing her to watch the destruction of family photographs; sometimes he went out alone for the evening having locked her in a room or tied her to the bed. As a result of his alcoholism, his career suffered: when the United States declared war on Germany in 1917, he was denied the chance to serve in Europe, and put in command of an air training station in California; when the war ended, he was relegated to a desk post at the Navy Department in Washington. His frustration at these unheroic jobs led to a further deterioration of his personality. Wallis endured the nightmare stoically until, in the autumn of 1921, after a night during which he had abused her both verbally and physically and then locked her in a hotel bathroom, she could stand no more. She left him to return to her mother, who was now living in Washington. Her first thought was to seek a divorce; but her family persuaded her that such a course would bring social disgrace, and so for the next few years she lived the life of a married woman living apart from her husband, who agreed to allow her $225 a month out of his navy pay.

Having escaped from her torment, Wallis was determined to enjoy life in

Above Wallis (second from left), Win (second from right) and friends
soon after their marriage in 1916.

Below With Charlie Chaplin in 1920 in the grounds of the Hotel del Coronado; the two
women on the outside of the group are daughters of Rear-Admiral William Fullman.

Above Winfield Spencer as a naval cadet, about 1914.

Right At Coronado, California, where Win (below) commanded a naval air training station from 1918 to 1920.

Washington, where she had been able to make several well-connected friends. In spite of her miserable domestic life, her years as a navy wife had given her a certain worldliness and social confidence. She was lively and witty; she knew how to make herself attractive to men; and soon she was much in demand as an 'extra woman' at diplomatic parties in the federal capital. She was elected to the Soixante Gourmets, a fashionable dining club whose leading light was her friend Wilmott Lewis, the witty Washington correspondent of the London *Times*. She had at least one serious, indeed tempestuous, love affair at this period – with Felipe Espil, the debonair Secretary to the Argentine Embassy (later Argentine Ambassador to the United States). They considered marriage, though for reasons which are not clear, he decided to marry someone else. (Divorce was evidently not the problem, for the woman Espil did marry had been divorced twice.)

Early in 1924 Wallis travelled to Europe for the first time, visiting Paris with her recently widowed (but still youthful) cousin Corrine. They had a wonderful time, particularly after befriending two diplomats at the United States Embassy who acted as their escorts and guides. Wallis was considering applying for a divorce there when she received a letter pleading for a reconciliation from Winfield Spencer, now commanding an American gunboat at Hong Kong. She sailed out to join him that July; but after a brief second honeymoon he returned to his old ways – even forcing her to accompany him to the Chinese brothels he frequented – and so she left him for good. But China fascinated her, and she was in no hurry to return to America. With a vague idea (soon abandoned) of getting a divorce from the American court there, she went to stay in Shanghai, where she made the acquaintance of a jovial English business-man named Robbie. In his company she spent several enchanting weeks, attending garden parties and race meetings, and whirling around the ballroom of the Majestic Hotel to the strains of the new dance melody *Tea for Two*.

In the late autumn of 1924 she decided to move on to Peking. This was adventurous, since four rival generals and their armies were competing for con-trol of the capital, which was also at war with the break-away Kuomintang Republic in the South. But she longed to see the glories of the imperial city, and had learnt that Gerry Greene, the diplomat who had recently 'squired' her in Paris, was now First Secretary at the American Legation. During the rail journey her train was repeatedly stopped and boarded by soldiers and bandits, but Wallis managed to avoid their attentions by assuming an air of freezing indifference. Soon after her arrival, at a hotel dance to which she had been taken by Greene, she ran into a friend, Kitty Bigelow, a navy widow who had recently married as her second husband Herman Rogers, a handsome and wealthy New Englander who had been lured to China by intellectual and artistic interests. Wallis accepted their invitation to stay with them at their house in the Tartar City, and for some months they lived as a *ménage à trois*, together exploring that fascinating metropolis, as yet little changed from Manchu times, and spending their weekends at a temple in the hills. Wallis developed a close (though platonic) relationship with Herman, who in 1936 would write to her that she had always been his 'one example of a perfectly wise and complete person'. As she candidly confesses in her memoirs, she also lost her heart to other Europeans in Peking – 'there was a dashing British military officer and a gallant Italian naval officer who whirled briefly in and out of my life'.

During the Abdication Crisis, it was rumoured that Wallis practised unusual sexual 'arts' which she had picked up in China; there was even said to be a secret file, personally commissioned by King George V, giving details of her practices and how she had acquired them. (According to Philip Ziegler in his official biography of Edward VIII, no copy of such a document exists in any official archive, nor has anyone gone on record as having actually seen it.) These arts, generally described as involving some clutching power of the vagina, were said to explain the 'hold' she exercised over King Edward. Certainly, Wallis was always strongly interested in men, and she doubtless discovered various ways of giving them pleasure; but it is unlikely that those ways involved acts of vaginal intercourse, nor did she need to go to China to learn them.

In the late spring of 1925 serious anti-European rioting broke out in China. Caught up in various incidents, Wallis displayed her usual courage, but was made aware that there was little future for her in China, that it was time to bring her oriental idyll to an end. And so she sailed for home that summer after 'what was without doubt the most delightful, the most carefree, the most lyrical interval of my youth – the nearest thing to a lotus-eater's dream that a young woman brought up the "right" way could expect to know'. She became seriously ill during the sea voyage, and lay in hospital at Seattle for some weeks: this

Wallis in China, 1924–5. During her adventurous year there, she formed a close friendship with Herman (opposite in bathing suit) and Katherine Rogers (below), with whom she went to live in Peking. She also had romantic affairs with several men, including the dashing Italian Naval Attaché, Alberto da Zara (opposite with Wallis at the races).

SHANGHAI
RACE CLUB

COMPLIMENTARY
MEMBER'S BADGE

Spring Race Meeting, 1925
This Ticket is only issued by the
Authorisation of the Stewards

Name *Mrs Spencer*

No. *244*

was the first indication of the stomach trouble that would plague her intermittently for the rest of her life, culminating in a collapse fifty years later which would reduce her to a bedridden invalid.

Wallis was now determined to put an end to her moribund marriage. Having discovered that the State of Virginia offered a relatively simple divorce to anyone who had resided there for two years, she went to live at a hotel at Warrenton, a sleepy country town in the foothills of the Blue Ridge Mountains. It had the advantage of being quite near both to Washington, where she was able to visit her mother and resume her old social life, and to the estate of her rich cousin Lelia, an important personality. There Wallis led a simple life, playing golf (which she did indifferently) in the afternoons and poker (at which she excelled) in the evenings. Her best friend in the town was a young bank clerk, Hugh Spilman. Interviewed years later, he recalled that Wallis 'was a devil, but . . . good company – _wonderful_ company! Always up to something. She was invited out a lot because she could make a party go. . . . I don't mind admitting that I was pretty crazy about her, even though she was an awful flirt. . . . '

Wallis varied her life in Virginia by visiting New York, where she stayed with her old schoolfriend Mary Kirk and her French husband, Jacques Raffray. It was there, in 1926, that she met the Raffrays' friend Ernest Simpson. The only son of a successful English shipping broker (who was a converted Jew) and an American mother, Ernest was a year younger than Wallis and like her in the process of disentangling himself from an unhappy marriage. He was something of a misfit, conscious of his mixed ancestry and not quite sure whether he was British or American. During the First World War, he had given up his studies at Harvard to go to England and train for a commission in the Coldstream Guards. At the time he met Wallis he was running the New York office of the family firm. In her memoirs Wallis was always generous to Ernest, who was then still alive. 'Reserved in manner, yet with a gift of quiet wit, always well-dressed, a good dancer, fond of the theatre, and obviously well-read, he impressed me as an unusually well-balanced man.' They quickly became friends, though 'the friendship was for a long time no more than one of those casual New York encounters between the extra man and the out-of-town woman who find pleasure in each other's tastes'.

In 1927 Wallis visited Italy and France as the companion of her Aunt Bessie, who paid for the trip out of a legacy. As always, it was thrilling for her to see new places and she made many new friends. She was in Paris in October when she learned of the sudden death of her Uncle Sol. In his will (which was successfully challenged by his relations) that dour bachelor bequeathed the bulk of his estate, valued at five million dollars, to set up a home for indigent gentlewomen in memory of his mother. Wallis, once thought to have been his principal heiress, was left the income from a fund of $15,000, to cease in the event of her remarriage.

A few weeks later Wallis received her divorce decree at Warrenton. Ernest, who was about to be transferred to his firm's London office, immediately proposed to her. To reflect on his proposal, she accepted an invitation from Herman and Kitty Rogers to stay with them at Lou Viei, the secluded villa near Cannes where, having left China, they had recently gone to live. Wallis was in no hurry to accept Ernest, who was her opposite in many ways – dull and conventional whereas she was lively and adventurous. But he offered her something she had come to value – security. After five tormented years with Winfield Spencer, followed by six amusing but rootless years as a single woman, there was much to be said for the bourgeois comforts and homely virtues of life with the solid and predictable Ernest.

Having made up her mind, Wallis joined Ernest in London, seeing that city for the first time. From there she wrote to her mother in Washington on 15 July 1928, in a tone which can only be described as one of resignation.

I've decided definitely that the best and wisest thing for me to do is to marry Ernest. I am very fond of him and he is *kind* which will be a contrast. . . . Mummie I shall miss having you with me terribly but the second time doesn't really seem so important. . . . I'm sure I shall be lonely next winter and homesick. However, I can't go on wandering for the rest of my life and I really feel so tired fighting the world alone and with no money. Also 32 doesn't seem so young when you see all the really fresh youthful faces one has to compete against. So I shall just settle down to a fairly comfortable old age. . . . I hope this hasn't upset you darling – but I should think you would feel happier knowing somebody was looking after me. All my love to you – and do send wishes for success this time.

Wallis married her second husband Ernest Simpson at a registry office
in London on 21 July 1928.

For whatever reason, Alice was indeed upset by the marriage: in her letters to Wallis during the months that followed, she did not once enquire after her son-in-law. A year later she died after suffering a stroke, aged only fifty-nine, but worn out after a life of drudgery with which her upbringing had not equipped her to deal. Wallis longed to avenge her mother by doing something interesting with the rest of her life: in her present circumstances this essentially meant striving after social success in London. The only member of her family to whom she still felt close was her Aunt Bessie, with whom she promised to keep in touch: her letters to that cherished relative during the next few years would be the chronicle of an extraordinary tale.

On their honeymoon in Spain.

An infra-red photograph of the Prince of Wales and friends watching a film at a London cinema in 1934. The *Daily Mail*, which printed the picture, noted that Lady Queensberry sat on the Prince's right and Lady Portarlington on his left, but did not identify the next two figures in the row – Wallis Simpson, with whom the Prince had recently fallen in love, and her husband Ernest.

CHAPTER TWO

'What a treat . . . to meet the Prince'

1929–34 **T**hough Wallis cannot be said to have been in love with Ernest Simpson, they soon developed a cosy, affectionate relationship. The element of non-consummation would not have worried Ernest, who sought a wife who could provide companionship and organize his domestic and social existence. His letters to her are like those of a brother to a sister. They began married life in London in affluent circumstances: Ernest's business was booming, while Wallis received some unexpected capital from the unravelling of her Uncle Sol's complicated will. She discovered that one could live better in England than in America on an equivalent income. For a year they rented a large town house in Marylebone, fully furnished and staffed. At the end of 1929 they acquired a flat of their own in a fashionable, solidly-built new block in the same neighbourhood, Bryanston Court. Wallis had a splendid time decorating and furnishing it, which she did with originality and style: she had a good eye, and had already developed a talent for creating a comfortable and well-run establishment with a pleasant atmosphere. The flat was not particularly large, and somewhat lugubrious, but she found ways of making it warm and welcoming. She also efficiently managed her excellent domestic staff, consisting of a cook and two maids, hired after a long and careful search.

At the outset of her marriage, Wallis was lonely in London. Ernest had no close friends apart from his fellow guardsman Bernard Rickatson-Hatt, Editor-in-Chief of Reuters; and though his much older married sister, Maud Kerr-Smiley, had good social connections, she and Wallis did not get on. For a while their social life largely consisted of entertaining Ernest's business clients. However, by a lucky chance, Wallis's cousin Corrine arrived in London with her second husband George Murray, who had been appointed Assistant Naval Attaché at the United States Embassy. Soon the Simpsons had a social circle

Above Wallis and Ernest at a race meeting (left) and holidaying in Tunisia with their Romanian friend Georges Sebastian.

Below The drawing room of 5 Bryanston Court, the London flat acquired by the Simpsons in 1929 where Wallis made her first foray into the world of interior decoration. The principal colourings were lime green, pale apricot and faded browns.

based on the Embassy and the American business community in London. Among this rather limited group Wallis acquired a reputation as a hostess, known for her delicious food and lively conversation. The circle steadily expanded, thanks to Wallis's gift for making friends. Like her husband, she was normally ambitious for the period in that she enjoyed getting to know the socially prominent. She was delighted, for example, to make the acquaintance of Lady Sackville, the American wife of a well-known English peer; and Ernest was equally delighted when they were invited to stay at Knole, the Sackvilles' magnificent Tudor seat in Kent.

One of the Embassy couples whom Wallis got to know in 1930 was Benjamin Thaw, the new First Secretary, and his wife Consuelo. 'Connie' was one of the three famous Morgan sisters, beautiful daughters of an American consul who some years earlier had filled the gossip columns with their social exploits; like the other sisters, she had lesbian leanings, and she seems to have taken a fancy to Wallis. Another sister, Thelma, Viscountess Furness, a glamorous socialite who saw little of her husband, had recently become the mistress of the Prince of Wales, whom she had invited to spent the second weekend of January 1931 at her country house at Melton Mowbray in Leicestershire. Connie was also due to be there in the role of chaperone; but a few days before the party she was called away to the bedside of her ailing mother-in-law. To Wallis's astonishment Connie asked if she would stand in for her, travelling down by train with Ernest and Benjamin Thaw. Wallis was in the throes of a heavy cold, and nervous at the prospect of meeting the heir to the throne; but Ernest would not hear of their refusing, and so they went.

Edward, Prince of Wales, known to his intimates as David, eldest son and heir of the reigning King George V and Queen Mary, was then thirty-six. He was idolized by all classes on account of his romantic good looks, his gallant service in the First World War, his common touch, his concern for poverty and suffering, his role as a setter of fashion and style, and the star quality which had been so evident on the spectacular (though strenuous) overseas goodwill tours he had undertaken throughout the 1920s. What was known only to an inner circle was that he could be irritable, selfish and stubborn, and felt deeply oppressed by his official life and family pressures, from which he sought escape in the frenetic pursuit of pleasure. From his mid-twenties onwards he had enjoyed a long string of casual affairs with women, as well as a serious and

Born in 1894, Edward, Prince of Wales became heir to the throne on the accession of his father, King George V, in 1910. With his good looks, his great charm and his sympathy with the common man, he developed into one of the popular heroes of the day. Only a few were aware of his melancholia, his restless quest for pleasure and his often thoughtless behaviour. *Above left* As a boy. *Above right* During the First World War, when he won the hearts of British troops. *Left* On his tour of India in 1922, as Colonel-in-Chief of Jacob's Horse. *Opposite above* With his younger brother Prince George (left), and the British Prime Minister Stanley Baldwin and wife, on a tour of Canada in 1925. *Opposite left* Drawing by Rothenstein, 1929. *Opposite right* A card bearing this heart-throb photograph was available to purchasers of Yardley's Old English Lavender Soap.

In a postscript to her aunt dated 13 January
1931, Wallis signalled her first meeting,
three days earlier, with the Prince of Wales.
'I never finished the letter as Friday I got up
and spent the entire day on hair and nails
etc. as Saturday we were going to Melton
Mowbray to stay with Lady Furness (Mrs
Thaw's sister) and the Prince of Wales was
also to be a guest. . . . It was quite an experience. . . .'

enduring romantic relationship with Freda Dudley Ward, the wife of an MP.

The Prince's first encounter with his future wife took place at Melton Mowbray on the evening of Saturday 10 January 1931, when (as he recalled twenty years later) they had a lively talk about the differences between the British and American ways of life. Otherwise, he does not seem to have paid much attention to the Simpsons, who for their part felt ill-at-ease in a company whose main interest was horses. There can be no doubt, however, that both Ernest and Wallis were thrilled to have met the heir to the throne. There was an element of romantic snobbery in the attitude of Ernest, who revered royalty, whereas Wallis's main feeling was a schoolgirlish delight at having made contact with one of the great stars and heart-throbs of the day. 'You can imagine what a treat it was to meet the Prince in such an informal way', she wrote to Aunt Bessie. 'It was quite an experience and as I've made up my mind to meet him ever since I've been here, I feel relieved.' She was pleased that the encounter had made her patronizing sister-in-law jealous, but wanted to keep it secret from her friends in America for a while. She wondered if she would ever see the Prince again: just a few days after his visit to Melton, he left on a four-month tour of South America, designed to promote British trade there.

The meeting acted as a spur to Wallis's social ambition. She arranged to be presented at Court during the coming London season. She made other glamorous new acquaintances, including Thelma's twin sister Gloria Vanderbilt and her Russian-born friend Nada, Marchioness of Milford Haven. 'It is nice for us to meet all these swell people', she wrote to her aunt on 16 April, 'even if we can't keep up their pace!' Most of her life was still humdrum, consisting of running her small household and exchanging hospitality with her middle-class friends; but she was excited at the prospect of extending her social horizons.

On 15 May Thelma invited the Simpsons to a cocktail party for the Prince, who had just returned from Argentina. (Also a guest, to Ernest's annoyance, was Felipe Espil, the Argentine diplomat who had been Wallis's lover in Washington eight years earlier.) To their surprise the Prince, exhibiting his famous royal memory, recognized the Simpsons and greeted them charmingly. Then, on 10 June, Wallis, having borrowed the required formal dress from Thelma and Connie, was presented at Court, going through the picturesque ceremony which then marked the official entry of a debutante into society. As she approached the royal thrones to make her curtsy to the King and Queen,

Just a few days after his casual encounter with Wallis in Leicestershire, the Prince of Wales, accompanied by Prince George, set out on his last great overseas tour, to promote British trade in South America. *Above left* The Prince on the outward sea journey. *Above right* The two Princes in Buenos Aires. *Below* A golfing party in Argentina. *Opposite* This Argentine cartoon alludes to the Prince's habit of shaking hands with his left hand when he had exhausted his right. His damaged right hand here symbolizes the Ottawa Agreement, under which London erected tariff barriers which threatened Anglo-Argentine trade.

CARAS Y CARETAS

DESPEDIDA CORDIAL

Príncipe de Gales. — Perdone que
no pueda darle la mano derecha.
Roca. — Yo tampoco.

Wallis in formal dress (borrowed from Thelma Furness and Connie Thaw) for her Presentation at Court on 10 June 1931. She wrote to her aunt: 'I was a bit nervous while waiting my turn but not during the actual "bobbing" to the King and Queen. After Court we went to Thelma Furness' for a party. The Prince was there and took Ernest and self home in his car at 3 a.m. which threw the porters into a gale. . . .'

she noticed the Prince of Wales and heard him remark to a neighbour that the lighting made all the women look ghastly. Afterwards Thelma gave another party to which the Simpsons were again bidden. The Prince complimented Wallis on her appearance, to which she smartly replied: 'But Sir, I understood that you thought we all looked ghastly!' He was enchanted by such irreverence, and ended by taking the Simpsons home in his car at three in the morning. Wallis was thrilled, particularly as the Prince was recognized by the porters at Bryanston Court, as a result of which the news was soon all over the building. 'I hope to have HRH here for a cocktail some afternoon', she wrote to her aunt; but it would be another six months before she saw him again.

In July 1931, Wallis, leaving her husband behind, went on holiday to Cannes together with the sisters Connie Thaw and Gloria Vanderbilt and their friend Nada Milford Haven. This seems to have been something of a lesbian jaunt, Gloria sharing a room with Nada and Wallis with Connie: the Gloria-Nada liaison, witnessed by the hotel staff, was to provide evidence three years later in the sensational Vanderbilt Baby Case, in which it was alleged that Gloria was morally unfit to bring up her daughter. With her somewhat masculine appearance and personality, Wallis was attractive to lesbians, but she does not seem to have been altogether comfortable in such society and left the party early to return to Ernest in London.

After all the social excitements of the first half of 1931, the autumn of that year was gloomy for the Simpsons. They were beginning to experience financial difficulties, for Ernest's shipping agency was suffering badly from the world recession, while the American stock market collapse had virtually wiped out the value of Wallis's investments. They had to give up their car and driver, and cut back on entertainment. Wallis was also unwell and had to have her tonsils out: as she lay in hospital recovering from what had turned out to be quite a serious operation, she was visited every day by the devoted Connie Thaw.

Shortly before Christmas Wallis met the Prince again at Connie's, and persuaded him to dine at Bryanston Court in the New Year. She wrote to her aunt that the dinner party at the flat had carried on until four a.m. – 'so I think he enjoyed himself'. The Prince returned the Simpsons' hospitality by inviting them to spend the last weekend of January 1932 at Fort Belvedere, a grace-and-favour residence at Sunningdale near Windsor, in the form of a miniature castle, which he used as a country retreat. It was close to his heart, for in the two years since he had moved there he had transformed the Fort (as he called it) from an ancient crumbling structure into a comfortable modern house, and the grounds from a wilderness into an imaginative garden. It was a place to which he could escape with his friends from the pressures of official life. The Simpsons were enchanted by the charm and informality of the Fort, where Thelma acted as hostess. With her interest in interior decoration, Wallis was particularly fascinated by the improvements and embellishments the Prince had made, and encouraged him to talk about them.

With help from Ernest, Wallis sent the Prince a letter of thanks in verse:

> Our week-end at Fort Belvedere
> Has left us both with memories dear
> Of what in every sense must be
> Princely hospitality. . . .

But once more it would be many months before they met again. The year 1932 was marked by continuing money worries and another breakdown in Wallis's health – this time a recurrence of the stomach trouble that had plagued her since her return from China in 1925. She did however get to know Thelma better. This resulted in further invitations to the Fort, where Wallis stayed, generally with her husband, half a dozen times the following autumn and winter. It was evident that her company amused the Prince.

On 29 January 1933 Wallis wrote a letter to Aunt Bessie from the Fort, which illustrates how familiar she was becoming with that house and its inhabitants. For the second week-end running she had gone down there with Thelma while Ernest was in Italy on business. 'It is cold for England now and . . . we have been skating out on the water with the Duke and Duchess of York. Isn't it a scream?. . . The Prince presented Thelma and self with skates. . . . I am writing . . . in the drawing room, the Prince doing *needle work* and 'Pops' [Thelma] reading aloud, my boy (or the one asked for me), 'Fruity' Metcalfe, having developed flu. . . . I can't stand the Morgan voice so asked permission to write to you during the reading. . . .' This was probably the first of Wallis's few meetings with the Duke and Duchess of York, who were to become King George VI and Queen Elizabeth and would greatly disapprove of her.

In March 1933 Wallis visited America for the first time since her mother's

(a) February 1932: Wallis tells her aunt that the Prince, after dining at Bryanston Court, had invited the Simpsons to their first week-end at Fort Belvedere. (b) The Prince at the Fort, which he came to love 'as I loved no other material thing'. After taking possession in 1929, he devoted most of his spare time to restoring the house and creating a garden. (c) An aerial view, showing the swimming pool terrace on the right and the battery of cannon in the foreground (which until 1907 had been fired on ceremonial occasions by a resident bombadier). Though it looked imposing from a distance, the Fort, built in the 1760s and enlarged in the 1820s, was a miniature fortress with tiny rooms and an intimate atmosphere.

(a)

(b)

(c)

death, a trip made possible thanks to Aunt Bessie's generosity. On the outward sea voyage she received a telegram from the Prince wishing her a good journey and speedy return, ensuring that she was treated with flattering respect by the ship's company. In her memoirs she says Ernest accompanied her; but her memory was wrong on this point, and indeed she appears to have relished the opportunity to escape from their humdrum life together and have a fling. On her return journey she wrote to Aunt Bessie (17 May) thanking her effusively for the trip, during which she had 'collected four men who never leave me be. Certainly I have [had] something this trip I'll never have again'. She had acquired a new suitor in the form of the ship's purser who had exchanged her cabin for a better one. 'It is going to take a bit of discipline to settle down to the domestic type again especially as I know it really was my swan song unless I can hang on to my figure and take a trip before I'm 40 which is only 3 years off.'

Wallis's absence seems to have increased the Prince's eagerness for her company. A few days after her return, she wrote to her aunt that 'we have spent the week-end at the Prince's and then have been to the Embassy Club Monday and Tuesday with him. Thelma is still the Princess of Wales. . . .' Two weeks later she wrote that they had spent Whitsun at the Fort. 'Prince George [the future Duke of Kent], Grand Duke Dmitri and wife were the party. It was fun but a touch too royal.' An International Conference took place in London, and she arranged with Thelma for the Prince to meet the American delegates whom she knew from her Washington period. The 19th of June was Wallis's birthday, which she celebrated 'at a restaurant on the river where the Prince met us after a very gay dinner. We went back to his house and made whoopee until 4.30. . . .' Four days later was the Prince's birthday, and Wallis gave him a silver matchbox-holder engraved with his cypher, accompanied by a short, formal letter to him which he preserved. On 4 July she gave an 'American dinner' for him at Bryanston Court.

Wallis and Ernest spent August and September 1933 in Norway on a business trip extended into a holiday; but as soon as they returned, they were asked to the Fort for the weekend. By now, such visits were so routine that Wallis hardly bothered to mention them to her aunt. She did however report with amusement (29 October) that Thelma and the Prince had turned up while she was entertaining two female cousins from Virginia. 'He stayed until 3 a.m. and

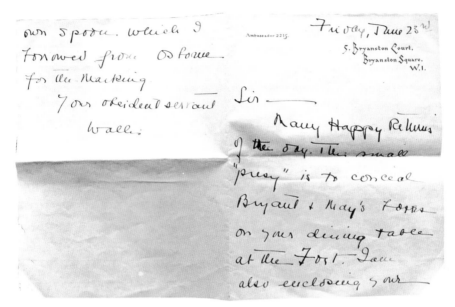

Wallis's first known letter to the Prince, on the occasion of his thirty-ninth birthday, 23 June 1933. Their affair had not yet begun and she was careful to employ the correct forms of address. Her present to him was a silver match-box holder (Bryant & May being a well-known brand of matches): in order to engrave this with his cypher, she had borrowed one of his spoons from Osborne, the butler at the Fort.

played the bag pipes for them and stood on his head and gave Madge a book of war pictures that he had intended for Ernest. . . . Madge and Lelia looked like two frightened rabbits when they came in.' Her letters continued to dwell on the financial crisis of the household. 'I think . . . requests for our society will lessen as we will not be able to entertain in return. . . . Thelma takes us to so many night clubs & that means new evening dresses. . . .' Thelma invited Wallis to a party with Noël Coward and another with Maurice Chevalier.

On New Year's Day 1934 Wallis wrote to her aunt that they had stayed up with the Prince's party until half past five in the morning, and that in the evening she would be giving a dinner for him at Bryanston Court, after which he would be taking them to the Chelsea Arts Club Ball. Thelma had given her three rings for Christmas, and the Prince a table for her drawing room. Soon afterwards Thelma left to spend two months in America. Before departing she asked Wallis (as both women recalled in their memoirs) to 'look after' the Prince in her absence. On 26 January Wallis wrote to Aunt Bessie that she was 'feeling lost' with Thelma in America, and that the Prince 'will miss her terribly'. Wallis and Ernest had spent the past weekend at the Fort; 'tried my best to cheer him up', she wrote. The following Wednesday he had dined at Bryanston Court, afterwards taking the Simpsons to Quaglino's.

The Prince had now known Wallis for three years, and had evidently come to like her immensely. She appealed to him because of her sense of fun, her forthrightness and her domesticity. She was obviously an amusing person to include in the late-night parties which were a feature of his social life. She treated him as a normal human being, and he felt comfortable with her. But he had not yet shown any signs of infatuation with her. After all, she was Thelma's friend, and happily married to Ernest. According to the Duke of Windsor's memoirs, the moment he began to see her in a different light was when, returning to London exhausted one night in February 1934 after a harrowing tour of working men's clubs in Yorkshire, he asked her to join a party he was giving at a London hotel; to his surprise she insisted on his telling her all about his tour. Here, he suddenly felt, was a woman who understood and shared his concerns and could soothe his brow, and he asked if they might meet more often.

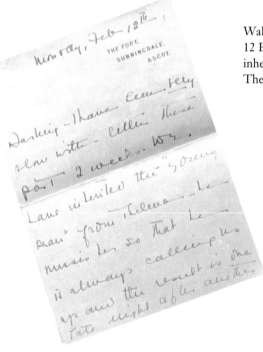

Wallis to her aunt from the Fort, 12 February 1934. 'We have inherited the "young man" from Thelma. . . .'

In fact, he seems in a very short time to have become addicted to her company. On 12 February Wallis wrote to her aunt from the Fort: 'We have inherited
the "young man" from Thelma. He misses her so that he is always calling up
and the result is one late night after another – and by late I mean 4 a.m. Ernest
has cried off a few but I have had to go on. I am sure the gossip will now be
that I am his latest. However he is very sweet and we have been able to have
some of our friends invited here. . . .' A week later she wrote from Bryanston
Court that 'the Prince . . . is here most of the time or telephoning 2 or 3 times
a day, being completely at a loose end. However Thelma will be back shortly. . . .'
She asked Aunt Bessie to send Thelma a dress to bring back to England for her,
and added in a postscript: 'It's all gossip about the Prince. I'm not in the habit
of taking my girlfriends' beaux. . . . I think I amuse him . . . and we like to
dance together – but I always have Ernest hanging around my neck so all is
safe.'

However, by the time Thelma returned to England at the end of March, the
Prince no longer had the same feelings for her. He greeted her coldly, and
rebuked her for having spent time in America with Prince Aly Khan, a notori-
ous rake. At the Fort Thelma noticed 'that the Prince and Wallis seemed to
have little private jokes. Once he picked up a piece of salad with his fingers:
Wallis playfully slapped his hand.' Thelma understood that Wallis had taken
literally her request to 'look after' the Prince. Despite Wallis's assurances that
she and the Prince were not having an affair, Thelma (who in any case had
probably tired of her role as his mistress) now left the Fort and the Prince's life
for good.

On 15 April Wallis wrote to Aunt Bessie from the Fort: 'We are still coming
here I suppose too much but of course it's tempting as one is so comfortable
and has such fun. Thelma is in Paris. I'm afraid her rule is over and I'm trying
to keep an even keel in my relations with HRH as he is very attentive at the
moment. And of course I'm flattered. . . .' A week later, she wrote from her flat:
'The Prince is here unless official things and there is Ernest and my friends the
other nights. You can well imagine I'm a bit worn – never a restful moment as
it takes great tact to manage both. . . . We never eat at home and of course
since I've produced PW several places we are filled with invitations from many
sources who have been quiet up to now. Wouldn't mother have loved it all?'

Wallis with Slipper, the cairn terrier the Prince gave her in November 1934.

CHAPTER THREE

'Perhaps it's only a boyish passion'

1934–36   *B*y the late spring of 1934, Wallis was established as the favourite of the Prince of Wales, who no longer wished to have any other women in his life. In his characteristically determined way, he had severed relations not only with Thelma Furness but also with Freda Dudley Ward, his close friend since 1919. With her love of adventure, Wallis was thrilled to occupy such a place in the affections of the Prince, whom she had already known for more than three years, and share something of the opulent and exciting life which surrounded him. It has been said that she was in love with the position rather than the man, but in fact, until the spring of 1936, she regarded her romance with him as a fairy tale which was bound to come to an end sooner or later. Throughout that time she was concerned not to allow her friendship with the Prince to destroy her marriage to Ernest, which unlike her royal idyll seemed to represent something solid and permanent.

On 25 April she wrote to her aunt that she hoped to go to Ascot with the Prince, provided 'he doesn't find another girl or return to Thelma and I can find the cash [for the clothes and tips] and also keep Ernest in good humour. At the moment he [Ernest] is flattered with it all and lets me dine once or twice a week with him *alone*.' This prompted Aunt Bessie to write sternly to her niece, warning her not to neglect her husband. 'You did give me a lecture', replied Wallis on 22 May, 'and I quite agree with all you say regarding HRH and if Ernest raises any objections to the situation I shall give the Prince up at once. So far things are going along beautifully and the 3 of us are always together in the little spare time PW has at this time of year.' She added that it was not true that she had 'taken the place' of Thelma – meaning presumably that her role in the Prince's life was not that of a mistress.

There has been endless speculation as to the nature of their relationship. It has been said that, owing to his inadequacies and her prowess, she was the first woman able to satisfy him sexually, which enabled her to establish a hold over him. This has been disputed by Philip Ziegler, who shows that the Prince enjoyed an active and apparently successful sex life up to the time he took up with Wallis. It is quite possible that the affair was not really sexual at all in the sense of being based on regular physical lovemaking. Winston Churchill wrote: 'He delighted in her company, and found in her qualities as necessary to his happiness as the air he breathed. . . . The association was psychical rather than sexual, and certainly not sensual except incidentally.' And Walter Monckton, the Prince's trusted adviser, wrote: 'No one will ever understand the story . . . who does not appreciate . . . the intensity and depth of his devotion to Mrs Simpson. To him she was the perfect woman. . . . It is a great mistake to assume that he was merely in love with her in the ordinary physical sense of the term. . . .' Lady Diana Cooper, who saw much of them together, believed they had a non-sexual relationship: she wrote that 'he worships her as a plaster saint'. This was certainly what the Duke of Windsor wanted the world to believe, for to the end of his life he violently rejected any suggestion that he had made love to his wife before their marriage: in the 1950s, he even threatened to sue Sir John Wheeler-Bennett for describing Mrs Simpson, in the first draft of his official biography of King George VI, as having been his 'mistress' in 1936.

Of course, it would be difficult to suggest that they did not enjoy a certain intimacy when alone together, or that such intimacy never led to sexual release. As Ziegler shows, there was much nudging and winking among courtiers and servants to do with lipstick stains, or the fact that he seemed something of a spent force ('limp and a rag') after long periods in her company. But any sexual activity was evidently subordinate to what would nowadays be called the role-playing side of their relationship. There can be no doubt that the Prince, who was immature in many ways, liked being treated as a little boy, and enjoyed being told off or told what to do. He also experienced (as a perceptive British diplomat who saw them together expressed it) 'an unsatisfied craving for domesticity'. With her natural bossiness and her love of domestic detail, Wallis appealed to something deep in his nature. The episode witnessed by Thelma, when Wallis admonished the Prince for eating a lettuce leaf with his fingers, set the tone for much that was to come. He was delighted when, as if by natural instinct, she started to take control of the domestic side of his life, planning his entertainments and buying his Christmas presents. He also willingly submitted to her reforming influence, for as Walter Monckton wrote: 'She insisted that he should be at his best and do his best at all times, and he regarded her as his inspiration.'

The Prince with Wallis at a night club.

It has often been said that Wallis played the role of a mother figure; but in a way she was also a father figure, for the Prince enjoyed being rebuked by her, and rebuke was something he had hitherto received from his father. The fact that she was not an ordinary woman, that she could possibly not be made love to in the way that he had made love to other women, may well have been part of her appeal and fascination for him: in Freudian terms, it is possible that she satisfied a subconscious homosexual urge.

Above In Biarritz, August 1934, with
Aunt Bessie and Hugh Lloyd Thomas,
the Prince's Assistant Private
Secretary.

Left At Portofino, September 1934.

Below Wallis's New Year message to
the Prince for 1935.

The Prince invited Wallis to join him on his summer holiday in 1934. She at first declined, as Ernest would be away on business and Aunt Bessie had planned to join her; but the Prince solved these problems by asking Aunt Bessie to join the party as chaperone. In early August the small party set out for Biarritz. After a few weeks of idle enjoyment there, they embarked on a cruise from Biarritz to Genoa on Lord Moyne's yacht *Rosaura*, during which they were joined by others, including Wallis's friends the Rogers. John Aird, the Prince's equerry, noted in his diary that the Prince followed her around 'like a dog'. Aird felt felt wary of her but had to admit she was a reforming influence – she made the Prince drink less and dress better. At the end of the holiday, Aird wrote that she 'does not seem to have any illusions [that the Prince would remain attached to her] and definitely does not want to do anything that will lose her husband'. Ernest did not seem to be unduly upset by his wife's jaunt, joking that she had been 'with Peter Pan on a trip to never-never land'. Meanwhile, the Prince told his private secretary that he had enjoyed the best holiday of his life. Towards the end of it he had presented her with a diamond-and-emerald charm for her bracelet, one of the first of many exquisite items of jewellery he was to give her.

In England that autumn life carried on as before, the Prince inviting himself to Bryanston Court and Wallis to the Fort. Wallis continued to be mindful of her husband, who was included in the royal invitations unless (as was frequently the case) he was abroad on business. When the Prince's favourite brother, George, Duke of Kent, married Princess Marina of Greece in November 1934, Wallis and Ernest were invited both to the ceremony at Westminster Abbey and the court ball at Buckingham Palace. At the ball, Wallis, wearing a tiara borrowed from Cartier, was presented by the Prince to the King and Queen, who were displeased, as they had not wished to invite the Simpsons, whose names had been surreptitiously added to the list at the last moment. The Prince continued to lavish presents on her: on 3 December Wallis wrote that he had presented her with a cairn puppy (a permanent reminder of her royal suitor, he was named Slipper but came to be known as 'Mr Loo'). On 30 December she wrote: 'The Prince has thank God been at Sandringham since last Monday which has been a lovely rest for us and especially me.' But he was going to see in the New Year with the Simpsons and then take them to Quaglino's. During this party Wallis, who during the autumn had already

As their relationship developed, the Prince and Wallis gave each other tiny inscribed charms, mostly made by Cartier in London, many in the form of bejewelled Latin crosses, others medallions of various shapes inscribed with handwriting, some representing small animals such as frogs or ladybirds. Wallis wore hers on a bracelet, the Prince wore his on a necklace. Some commemorate personal events while others refer to anniversaries. The earliest carries the date March 1934 while the last refers to a stomach operation Wallis underwent in New York in 1944. The entire collection was sold by Sotheby's in Geneva in 1987, along with the rest of the Duchess's jewellery, for the benefit of her heir, the Pasteur Institute.

(a)

(b)

(c)

(d)

Wallis, usually accompanied by Ernest and
Slipper, spent most week-ends at the Fort,
where she eventually acted as the Prince's
hostess. (a) The Prince, Wallis and
Katherine Rogers. (b) An outdoor lunch
party – the others are the Prince's old
friends Humphrey Butler (in dark suit) and
Colin Buist (in light suit), with their wives.
(c) Wallis, Ernest and others on the swimming pool terrace. (d) Wallis relaxing with
Slipper. (e) Wallis and the Prince in
Tyrolean costume, probably preparing for
their visit to Austria in February 1935.

(e)

The Prince inscribed this romantic studio portrait with the words: 'WE are too – 1935'.

received two more charms for her bracelet and a diamond hairpin, was presented with a brooch made up of two square emeralds.

The Prince invited Wallis to join him that February for winter sports at
Kitzbühel in Austria. His infatuation for her had already lasted for a year, and
seemed to grow by the day. Even Ernest was beginning to lose patience: when
she told him about the invitation (which included him), he stormed out of the
room, Wallis hearing him slam a door for the first time during their marriage.
The Prince's staff were also becoming worried by the affair, which they feared
was causing gossip and distracting him from his duties. But he would listen to
no-one, and Wallis duly accompanied him to Austria. She did not like skiing,
and found the resort dull as there was little else to do; but the party went on to
visit Vienna, Budapest and Paris, which she enjoyed immensely.

Around this time the Prince started writing Wallis short love-letters couched in a private language, and she responded in similar vein. They addressed each other in the third person as 'a boy' and 'a girl'. Collectively they called themselves WE in capital letters, a compound of the initials of Wallis and Edward and also probably a pun on the 'royal we'. Hence the motto 'God bless WE'. They used a number of invented words, such as 'eanum', meaning small and pathetic (oddly, this had been used by Ernest in his letters to Wallis). It was common for lovers at that period to write to each other in baby language, but the correspondence nevertheless reinforces the impression that, in his affair with Wallis, the Prince was realizing infantile desires and fantasies.

His early letters to her show that in 1935 he was already hinting at the possibility that they might marry in 1936. As he wrote to her from Cornwall in April 1935, sending her another jewel: 'This is not the kind of Easter WE want but it will be all right next year. . . . I love you more & more & more each & every minute & miss you *so* terribly here. . . . God bless WE.' In another (undated) letter of 1935, penned at the Fort in the middle of the night, he wrote to her:

> Oh! a boy does miss a girl here so terribly tonight. . . . *Please, please* Wallis don't get scared or lose faith when you are away from me. I love you more and more every minute and *no* difficulties can possibly prevent our ultimate happiness. . . . I do hate and loathe the present situation . . . and am just going mad at the mere thought . . . that you are alone there with Ernest. God bless WE forever my Wallis. You know your David will love you and look after you so long as he has breath in his eanum body.

That Wallis did not take these protestations too seriously, that she still valued her marriage, and that she found the Prince sometimes exasperating is revealed in a letter she wrote to him in the summer of 1935, after the Prince's self-centred behaviour over a period of days had provoked Ernest to an outburst of irritation.

> I was and still am most terribly upset. You see my dear one can't go through life stepping on other people. I know that you aren't really selfish or thoughtless but your life has been such that you have been the one considered so that quite naturally you think only of what you want and take it too without the slightest thought of others. . . . I had a long quiet talk with

In February 1935, Wallis accompanied the Prince on an Austrian skiing holiday – not a great success as she lacked an aptitude for athletic pursuits. 'Can't say I couldn't live without winter sports', she wrote to her aunt after her first skiing lesson. The others in the group are Bruce Ogilvy (equerry), his sister and sister-in-law, James Dugdale and Andrew Lyall.

E[rnest] last night and I felt very eanum at the end. Everything he said was so true. . . . Doesn't your love for me reach to the heights of wanting to make things a little easier for me? . . . Sometimes I think you haven't grown up . . . and perhaps it's only a boyish passion. . . . Your behaviour last night made me realise how very alone I shall be some day – and because I love you I don't seem to have the strength to protect myself from your youthfulness. God bless WE and be kind to me in the years to come for I have lost something noble for a boy who may always remain Peter Pan.

Meanwhile, Wallis continued to lead her double life as Ernest's wife and the Prince's companion. June 1935 saw the Silver Jubilee of King George and

Left At Ascot, June 1935.

Below First page of Wallis's admonishing letter to the Prince.

Queen Mary, and the Prince ensured that both Wallis and Ernest were included in the many festivities. He was able to invite them to the reception at Buckingham Palace after solemnly assuring his father that Mrs Simpson was not his mistress. (Courtiers scoffed at what they saw as a barefaced lie – but it is not unreasonable to suppose he was telling the truth.) Even when he was absent that summer attending a naval review in the English Channel, the Prince thought constantly of Wallis. From HMS *Faulknor* he sent her the following telegram *en clair*: 'I feel so eanum not having talked to you today. Are you missing me as much as I am you?'

Wallis now had an almost recognized social status as the Prince's favourite, and found herself showered with invitations from prominent English people, as well as the grandest Americans visiting London. 'It is very amusing what one is invited to in hopes of PW [coming also]', she wrote to Aunt Bessie on 29 June. 'All the best titles come across whereas no-one noticed Mrs Simpson before. It's fun for once in one's life. . . .' Courtiers and old established families tended to be wary of her, but there were many who liked her, though she was generally considered an unusual friend for the Prince to have. Cecil Beaton, meeting her for the first time that summer, found her 'brawny and raw-boned in her sapphire-blue velvet', but 'liked her immensely' and thought her 'bright and witty and chic'. Harold Nicolson, meeting her with the Prince at the theatre, found her 'bejewelled, eyebrow-plucked, virtuous and wise' and 'clearly out to help him'. The politician and socialite Chips Channon (later an admirer) thought her 'jolly, plain, intelligent, quiet, unpretentious', and noted that she already walked into a room 'with the air of a personage'.

Although the British press, in accordance with the then-existing tradition of respecting the private lives of royalty, wrote nothing about Wallis, there was much comment in the American press, particularly in the Hearst newspapers, a fact which at this stage amused rather than irritated her.

As during the previous year, Wallis joined the Prince on his 1935 summer holiday, while Ernest went to America on business. 'Ernest will give you an outline of our life since royalty arrived', she wrote to her aunt. 'He thinks it all a great joke. And so it is but I never had so much fun before or things so easy and I might as well finish up any youth that is left to me with a flourish.' The Prince was now so strongly under Wallis's influence that she seems to have dictated the arrangements for the holiday, which began at a villa near Cannes.

Scenes from the summer holiday of 1935 in the South of France. The group on the boat is (left tro right) Lord Louis Mountbatten, Herman Rogers, Kitty Rogers, Wallis with Slipper.

Various notes she addressed to him there show the extent to which she had taken charge of his domestic life.

> David – Have the table moved back as far as possible and if the Vansittarts are coming there would be far more room for 10 if the Finn could produce chairs without arms. Here is a suggestion for seating. I would also have two sorts of cocktail and white wine offered as well as vin rosé, the servants to pour the wine. Also I didn't see a green vegetable on the menu. Sorry to bother you but I like everyone to think you do things well. Perhaps I'm quite fond of you! Do take V off after lunch and get the information we want. . . .

The 'information' sought from Vansittart, who was head of the Foreign Office, was whether the crisis resulting from Mussolini's designs on Abyssinia would affect their plans to cruise around Italy that September on the Duke of Westminster's yacht. The answer was that it would. As a result, they took the yacht only as far as Corsica, but at Wallis's suggestion the party went on to Austria and Hungary, which she had so enjoyed visiting the previous March. They ended up in Paris, where Wallis was able to order clothes at Mainbocher at half-price and have them sent to England in the Prince's aeroplane. The Prince managed to have her included in a lunch with Pierre Laval, the French Prime Minister.

Writing to her aunt at the end of October, Wallis said that she missed Ernest (who was still in America) but was leading a dizzy social life, receiving invitations from such people as Lord Sefton, Lady Diana Cooper, Lady Cunard and Lady Mendl. 'What a bump I'll get when some young beauty appears and plucks the Prince from me!' When she next wrote, in mid-November, she had little to say about Ernest, who had returned, but reported that she was shortly to dine with the Duke and Duchess of Kent and herself give a dinner for her new friend the Austrian Minister. 'I enjoy meeting all these people and sometimes it seems strange to think of the days of struggle in . . . the [Baltimore] flat where mother had the café and was forever working herself to death to give me things. I wonder if in any way I'll ever be able to reward her efforts? Or if my insatiable ambitions will land me back in a one room [Washington] flat on Connecticut Hill?'

On 9 December Wallis reported that she had lunched with Lady Oxford, the formidable widow of the Prime Minister Asquith, whom she had found 'terrifying'. She had invited the Kents to dinner at Bryanston Court but wondered how she was going to cope as she was without a housemaid. She had gone shopping to buy the Prince's Christmas presents, one hundred and sixty-five for his staff alone, and was now spending the weekend at the Fort wrapping them up. She did not mention Ernest at all, though quite possibly he was with her at the Fort. She seems to have assumed by this time that he would always be there, waiting for her in the background. As Ernest's friend Rickatson-Hatt later told the King's friend Monckton, 'her intention was to have her cake and eat it. She was flattered by the advances of the Prince of Wales and enjoyed his generous gifts to the full. She thought that she could have them and at the same time keep her home with Simpson.'

Meanwhile, that autumn, the Prince thought seriously about renouncing his rights to the throne to marry Wallis, in the (far from certain) event of her being willing and able to divorce Ernest. It is unlikely that he mentioned this to her in so many words, as she would have been horrified, though he continued to write her poetic love letters alluding to his dream of their coming union, which she must have regarded as a sort of literary device. However, the Prince could not bring himself to mention what he had in mind to his father, with whom he had always had tense and difficult relations. Had he done so, he might have found the King not unreceptive: for in January 1935, having been given reports of Wallis, George V had told Admiral Halsey, the Prince's Chief of Staff, that 'he was beginning to think it would almost be better if the Prince of Wales abdicated. . . .'

At Sandringham for Christmas 1935, the Prince almost broached the subject, but was deterred by the King's fragile health. 'It really is terrible here', he wrote to Wallis, 'and so much the worst Xmas I've ever had to spend with the family.' With the marriage of his brother the Duke of Gloucester a month earlier, he alone of the four brothers found himself without the comfort of a wife. By the New Year he was with Wallis again. 'Oh my Wallis, I know we'll have Viel Glück to make us *one* this year', he wrote to her just after they had seen in 1936 together. (A courtier, Alan Lascelles, later claimed that the Prince and Wallis had laid New Year plans to run away together early in 1936, but were foiled by events. It is possible that this was a pipe-dream of the Prince: it is impossible to believe that Wallis would have gone along with it.)

Above The four Princes – George, Duke of Kent; Edward, Prince of Wales; Albert, Duke of York; Henry, Duke of Gloucester. With the marriage of Prince George to Princess Marina in November 1934, and Prince Henry to Princess Alice in November 1935, only the Prince of Wales lacked the comforts of married life.

Left The Prince's New Year message to Wallis for 1936.

Two weeks later, Wallis was with him at the Fort when he received a letter from his mother saying that his father was not well at Sandringham. He promptly returned there, from where he wrote to her on 18 January:

My own Sweetheart,

Just a line to say I love you more and more and need you so to be with me at this difficult time. There is no hope whatever for the King, it's only a matter of how long, and I won't be able to get up to London tomorrow if he's worse. But I do long long to see you even for a few minutes my Wallis, it would help so much. Please take care of yourself and don't get a cold. You are all and everything I have in life and WE must hold each other so tight. It will all work out right for us. God bless WE. Your

DAVID

On the afternoon of 20 January, Wallis was with friends at the cinema when the celebrated bulletin of Lord Dawson, the royal physician, was read out that the King's life was drawing peacefully to its close. (In fact, Dawson was about to kill his monarch with a euthanasia injection.) Later that evening, while having supper with her friends, she received a telephone call from Sandringham with the news that George V had died. 'It was only as I hung up', she wrote in her memoirs, 'that I realized that David was now King.' Ernest immediately wrote a letter of sympathy to his new sovereign, pledging his loyalty.

Every Inch a King: Edward VIII as Colonel-in-Chief of the Seaforth Highlanders.

CHAPTER FOUR

'A tragedy he can't marry without loving'

JANUARY–AUGUST 1936 *T*he new reign began in an atmosphere of great excitement and hope. 'I think he will make a great King of a new era', wrote Wallis to her aunt, 'and I believe the country thinks the same.' But how far would her own position extend into the new era? She knew that, as sovereign, he was expected to marry suitably and produce an heir. For all her attachment to him, all the assurances of devotion he had given her, she still believed her days as the King's friend to be numbered. In her first letter to him after his accession to the throne, she wrote: 'Some day of course I must learn to be always alone . . . also I must develop strength to look at papers containing your photographs and accounts of your activities. . . . God bless you and make you strong where you have been weak.'

But the idea of giving her up was the last thought in the King's mind. He had always viewed his accession to the throne with a certain dread, and he acutely felt the loneliness and responsibility of his new position: now more than ever, he felt he simply could not do without her. The first weeks of the reign were busy ones, filled with ceremonies and formalities: but he telephoned her constantly, sent her flowers, called on her every evening at Bryanston Court, and spent every weekend with her at the Fort. 'I have had to be at the new King's beck and call', wrote Wallis to her Aunt Bessie on 30 January, 'being the only person he has to really talks things over with normally, and it has all been a great strain.'

Many of the King's entourage were frankly antagonistic to Wallis: they felt she was unsuitable to be the closest friend of the sovereign, and that, owing to his obsession with her and desire to be with her as much as possible, he was inclined to neglect his duties. But they did not, of course, express their views to Wallis; and although some of the King's long-standing aides tried to approach him on the subject, he made it clear that he would tolerate no criticism of her.

Above The new King, in the company of Wallis and his Assistant Private Secretary Alan Lascelles, watches his own proclamation from a window at St James's Palace.

Opposite The King walking with his brothers the Dukes of York and Gloucester in the funeral procession of George V.

(Indeed, two of them, Halsey and Trotter, found themselves suddenly retired, no doubt partly on account of their attitude towards her.) Wallis was therefore largely unaware of the feeling against her which existed at court. On the other hand, she was certainly aware of the many distinguished people in society and public life who flattered her by telling her how much they liked her and what a suitable and beneficial friend they considered her to be for the King. 'I am implored on all sides not to leave him', she wrote to her aunt, 'as he is so dependent on me and I am considered to be a good influence. . . . Of course I am very fond of him and proud and want him to do his job well and he is so lonely and needs companionship and affection, otherwise he goes wrong.'

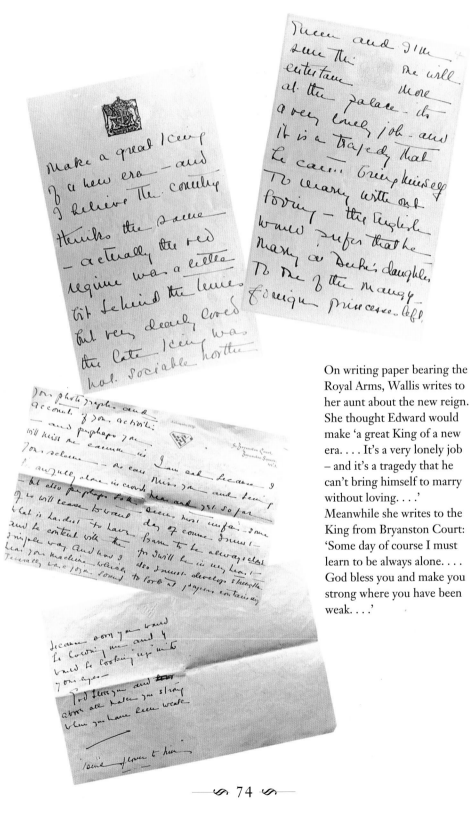

On writing paper bearing the Royal Arms, Wallis writes to her aunt about the new reign. She thought Edward would make 'a great King of a new era. . . . It's a very lonely job – and it's a tragedy that he can't bring himself to marry without loving. . . .'

Meanwhile she writes to the King from Bryanston Court: 'Some day of course I must learn to be always alone. . . . God bless you and make you strong where you have been weak. . . .'

One of Wallis's influences which everyone, even Queen Mary, agreed to be good was that she curbed his former heavy drinking. She also encouraged him to be more punctual and to attend to his official paperwork: paradoxically, because he wanted to be with her constantly he tended to be unpunctual and neglect his 'boxes'. As he came into his enormous inheritance as King, Wallis, with her keen instinct for household management, also encouraged him to think in terms of economy and the avoidance of waste. The King accordingly made various changes and cutbacks in the bloated traditional administration of the royal palaces and estates which, though mostly sensible and long overdue, caused widespread offence in his household and intensified the feeling against Wallis, who was perceived as being the inspiration for the reforms and on whom the King continued to lavish wonderful jewellery and other presents.

During the first months of his reign, the King was officially in mourning and accessible to few people; and Wallis was assiduously cultivated by politicians, senior civil servants and ambassadors who hoped to win her affections and impress her with their views and thus indirectly influence the King. For example,

The King with his two successors on the throne – his brother the Duke of York and ten-year-old niece Princess Elizabeth (seen here with her sister Margaret Rose, aged six).

we know that Vansittart at the Foreign Office hoped she would help to get royal support for the pro-Italian policy which he was trying to induce the Government to adopt. Wallis enjoyed being made up to by so many important people; but there is no evidence that she took advantage of her potentially powerful position – she knew little of politics, and did not have the make-up of a Lola Montes. 'I am asked to all small dinners in the official world, all sending messages via me', she wrote to her aunt. 'I'm just the same however and enjoying it all as a huge game – laughing a lot on the inside and controlling my tongue on the outside. . . . My life is not so free these days – that is in speech as I can't express any views as they then all think the King must have said [it]. . . .'

Wallis would undoubtedly have been only too happy to continue in her recognized and dignified role as the King's favourite, sharing his private life, discreetly sustaining him in his task, and enjoying all the social and material benefits that flowed from her position, until such time as he decided to marry, or felt he could do without her, whereupon she would retreat with her memories to the long-term security of her marriage to Ernest Simpson. But within a couple of weeks of his coming to the throne, the King was again talking obsessively of his desire to marry her, now with a view to her sharing the throne with him as Queen. As before, Wallis seems to have regarded this as a mere pipe-dream, flattering to her no doubt but hardly likely to be translated into reality. She wrote to him that he should 'cease to want what is hardest to have and . . . be content with the simple way'. To her aunt, she wrote (9 February): 'It's a very lonely job – and it's a tragedy that he can't bring himself to marry without loving.' The choice of a future bride seemed to be between a foreign princess and a British duke's daughter, but 'only the years and himself can arrange that for him'.

The King, however, was more than ever determined to make Wallis his consort. As Walter Monckton later wrote: 'He felt that he and Mrs Simpson were made for each other and that there was no other honest way of meeting the situation than by marrying her.' Shortly after coming to the throne, he resolved to remove the main obstacle in the way of his dreams – the Simpson marriage. And as Wallis showed no desire to put an end to that marriage, the King approached Ernest Simpson. This was a shrewd step, for the half-American Ernest had a sentimental reverence for the British monarchy, and was the King's to command. And while Wallis clung to her marriage, feeling it gave her security and respectability, the home-loving Ernest felt increasingly unhappy

On St David's Day, 1 March 1936, Edward VIII broadcast to his people: 'I am better known to you as the Prince of Wales. . . . And although I now speak to you as King, I am still that same man . . . whose constant effort it will be to promote the well-being of his fellow men. . . .' Much to his dismay, Wallis left him that day to spend two weeks in Paris, confused by his urgings that she divorce her husband and marry him.

about having to share her with the King: he had sought comfort with other women, including Wallis's old schoolfriend Mary Raffray, with whom he had begun an affair in New York in the late summer of 1935.

At the beginning of March 1936 – while Wallis herself was absent visiting dressmakers in Paris – a meeting took place between the King and Ernest at York House, which was witnessed by Ernest's best friend, the journalist Bernard Rickatson-Hatt. The result of this meeting was that Ernest reluctantly agreed to put an end to his marriage with Wallis, by giving her grounds for divorce, provided the King promised always to take care of her in future. Within a few weeks the King had kept his side of the bargain by settling an

Left The King and Ernest Simpson. While Wallis was in Paris, the King persuaded Ernest to agree to the divorce, promising in return that he would always look after her.
Right A country walk.

enormous sum of money on Wallis, enough to spare her financial worries for the rest of her life: the figure involved seems to have been about £150,000, amounting to about 15 per cent of the King's private fortune and equivalent to some £4 million in the values of 1996. (She returned most of this to him before the Abdication.) As for Ernest, he too kept his word: he invited his mistress Mary Raffray to come from America to make an extended visit to the Simpson flat in London, thus both providing Wallis with a pretext for divorce and removing any qualms she might have had about abandoning him.

What meanwhile of Wallis's feelings? When she first learnt of the King's meeting with Ernest, she seems to have felt a stab of anger. Writing to her aunt from Paris on 8 March, she confessed to a mood of 'rage, exhaustion and despair' and wrote of the King for the first time with a note of exasperation: 'That little King insists I return and I might as well with the telephone about four times daily – not much rest.' Soon afterwards, however, she was joined in

Paris by Ernest; and when she next wrote to her aunt a week later from the Fort, it was in quite a different tone. 'People must make their own lives, and . . . never having known security until I met Ernest, perhaps I don't get along well with it, knowing and understanding the opposite of it much better. . . .' Though the news of Mary Raffray's imminent arrival was something of a surprise, Wallis was glad she was coming as Ernest 'has always loved her. I suggest her to him as a future bride. . . .'

Mary arrived to stay with Wallis and Ernest at Bryanston Court on 24 March. For about two weeks, Ernest, Mary, Wallis and the King seem to have formed a *ménage à quatre*: they were together not only at the Fort, but when the King went to stay with his friend Lord Dudley at Himley Hall in Yorkshire. They went to various parties together, including a dinner given by Lady Cunard which was also attended by Ramsay MacDonald and the German Ambassador. Wallis seems to have had mixed feelings about the situation: she undoubtedly retained a fondness for Ernest and found it difficult to bear the sight of him conducting an open affair with one of her oldest friends (through whom indeed she had originally met him ten years earlier). 'I did everything in my power to give her a good time', she wrote to her aunt with a touch of (perhaps disingenuous) bitterness. 'However, she and Ernest stayed up most nights alone until 5 or 6 a.m. and finally went off quite calmly for three days in a hired motor. . . . Anyway it will all work out *beautifully* I hope. . . .'

On 4 May Wallis bared her heart to her aunt in a remarkable letter twenty pages long, in which she revealed that she and Ernest had agreed to separate in the near future. 'I have been under the most awful strain with Ernest and HM during the past year and a half. It is not easy to please, amuse, placate two men and to fit in to two such separate lives. . . . I cannot continue along the same lines, it is mentally and physically impossible, nor do the K and Ernest enjoy things as they are. . . . It would be extremely difficult to go back to life in Bryanston Court as it was before . . . I've outgrown both it and Ernest.' She knew that along with Ernest she would be losing the element of stability in her life; and even now, she could not imagine the King's feelings for her would last. At the end of the day, she expected to be 'comfortably off and to have had a most interesting experience, one that does not fall to everyone's lot. I have always had the courage for the new things that life sometimes offers.' For the moment, however, the King 'has another thing only on his mind' – presumably

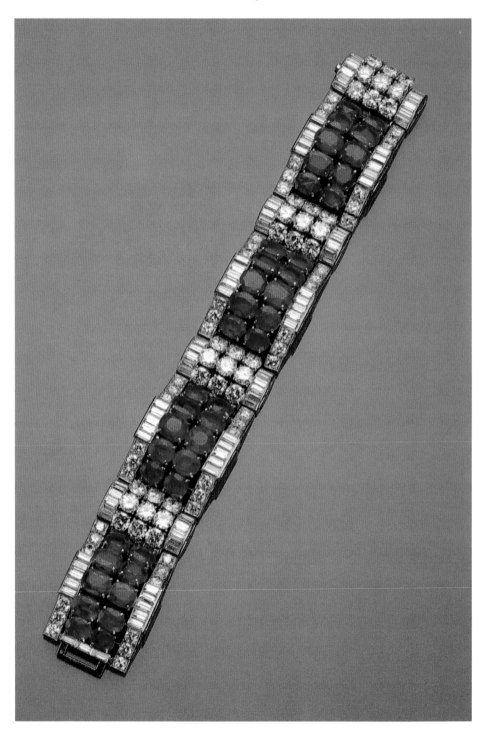

a reference to his marriage project. 'Whether I would allow such drastic action depends on many things and events and I should never allow him, if possible to prevent a rather stubborn character, to do anything that would hurt the country and help the socialists. In any case there is a new life before me whereas I can't go back to the old. . . . I have discussed all this with Ernest. Naturally he is sad but . . . he knows HM's devotion to me is deep and of the right sort. . . .'

This letter, dashed out spontaneously in a free-flowing hand, is suffused with a kind of euphoric fatalism. Wallis feels she must cut herself free of the past, represented by Ernest and Bryanston Court, and have the courage to see where her adventure with the King will lead her. As always, her main feeling is that it cannot last forever, that one day she will be alone (admittedly in comfortable circumstances) with her thrilling memories. Although she mentions the King's 'idea', she writes of it as a distant possibility, and as a factor which in the long run she will be able to control. She is indeed happy with her present role: 'Here they consider me important and my position is a good and dignified one.' Wallis writes that 'divorce I am not contemplating at the moment': her plan is merely 'to take a furnished house in the autumn and live alone for a while'.

Wallis's remark about not contemplating divorce is perhaps the one lie in the letter, for it was certainly something that the King never ceased to urge upon her, and during the month of June he arranged for her to consult his solicitor George Allen as to how she might put an end to her marriage before the Coronation took place in May 1937. On the other hand, there can be little doubt that she came to the decision to divorce Ernest with reluctance, that the King in effect pushed her into it. (This was later confirmed by her divorce solicitor Theodore Goddard to Lord Beaverbrook and others, as well as by Rickatson-Hatt who told Monckton that 'but for the King's obstinacy and jealousy, the affair would have run its course without breaking up the Simpson marriage'.) Indeed, after writing to her aunt on 4 May about her and Ernest's decision to separate, they in fact continued to live together at Bryanston Court

Opposite A bracelet of diamonds and Burmese rubies, by Van Cleef and Arpels, which the King gave Wallis when she finally submitted to his pressure and agreed to divorce her husband. It is inscribed _Hold Tight, 27.iii.36_ – a day that the King, Wallis, Ernest and Mary Raffray (Wallis's old friend who was now Ernest's mistress) all spent together at the Fort.

for eleven weeks – during which time Wallis suffered quite badly from her old stomach trouble, an indication of the tension and uncertainty under which she was living.

On 27 May the King gave the first formal dinner of his reign at his old bachelor apartments at York House, St James's Palace, where he was still living while Queen Mary moved out of Buckingham Palace. His seventeen guests included Wallis and Ernest, some friends of Wallis such as the Duff Coopers and Lady Cunard, and the Prime Minister Stanley Baldwin. ('Sooner or later, the Prime Minister must meet my future wife.') As had become usual by this time, Wallis, while not of course acting as hostess, made all the domestic arrangements for the party, such as planning the menus and table decorations and instructing the staff. The following day the names of the guests were published in the Court Circular, in which Wallis thus found herself mentioned for the first time since her Presentation at Court in 1931. Six weeks later, on 9 July, when the King gave his next dinner, Wallis's name appeared in the Circular without that of her husband (with whom however she was still living at Bryanston Court). This 'officialization' of her friendship with the King led to terrific gossip in London society. 'The Simpson scandal is growing', wrote Chips Channon, 'and she, poor Wallis, looks unhappy. The world is closing in around her, the flatterers, the sycophants, and the malice.'

The months of June and July were a frantic time for Wallis. She was busily involved in the season, attending parties in London, accompanying the King when he went to stay with the Duke of Marlborough at Blenheim Palace (Ernest coming too) and Lord Louis Mountbatten at Adsdean, and organizing his house party at the Fort for Ascot. At the same time, under constant pressure from the King, she was planning her separation from Ernest and discussing her forthcoming divorce with her solicitor Theodore Goddard. There must have been many moments when she regretted leaving Ernest; but he made things easier for her by continuing to conduct his affair with Mary Raffray in a fairly open manner in London. Owing to the cumbersome divorce laws of those days, the gentlemanly procedure was for the husband being divorced to 'furnish' the evidence by arranging to be 'discovered' in an adulterous situation at a hotel; and Ernest duly obliged by spending the night of 21 July with Mary at the Hôtel de Paris at Bray. A few days later he left Bryanston Court and the life of Wallis, whose solicitor proceeded to file her divorce petition.

The King photographed by Wallis on board Lord Louis Mountbatten's ship at Portsmouth, 1 July 1936.

Writing to her aunt on 1 August, Wallis gave no details of these domestic developments, but wrote of her state of exhaustion and mental turmoil. Her ulcer had given her trouble, though had now healed. Her social life was so complicated that she had taken on a secretary. She was besieged on all sides by people wanting favours of one sort or another. It had been difficult to plan for the future, though she hoped to take a furnished house in October and live there until after the Coronation. 'I have had a lot of tiresome business things to do and really feel the need of a holiday away from cares. . . . My job [*sic*] is too trying on the nerves for much relaxation – the tiny brain works overtime.' The King's summer plans had been complicated by the uncertain political situation in Europe, but they hoped to charter a yacht for a cruise in the Adriatic. 'I believe I leave here Saturday for a port on the Dalmatian coast. The name of the yacht is *Nahlin*. . . .'

On the *Nahlin* cruise, August 1936.

CHAPTER FIVE

'I am so anxious for you not to abdicate'

AUGUST–DECEMBER 1936   Since, owing to the continuing crisis over Abyssinia, it was thought inadvisable for the King to visit Italy, he and his party set out on 8 August to join the *Nahlin* at Sibernik in Yugoslavia. All the local dignitaries were there to see them off, along with thousands of peasants in local costume, who seemed as much intrigued by Wallis as by the King: she found this touching, not yet aware of the danger that the royal affair 'had become the property . . . even of the remote peasants of a faraway kingdom'. As they made their way down the Dalmatian coast, they encountered demonstrations of affection everywhere: in Dubrovnik, they were surrounded by a mob shouting 'Long live love'. 'We went ashore in a small, quaint town', wrote Wallis to her aunt, 'but even in that remote spot HM was recognised and the local militia had to be called out to deal with the crowd. Naturally it ruins exploring and closely resembles the Pied Piper.' The King seemed to revel in informality, ignoring the advice of his staff that he ought not to be seen by crowds wearing nothing but a pair of shorts: sometimes his behaviour brought a sharp rebuke from Wallis in front of other members of the party, to their embarrassment but doubtless his pleasure.

More by accident than design, the cruise helped stimulate pro-British feeling at a time when the Balkan states were under pressure from Italy and Germany. At Istanbul, their stop virtually became an official visit, the King being fêted by Atatürk and cheered by delirious crowds; only fourteen years earlier the British had been the hated occupiers of that city. At Sofia they were met by the King of Bulgaria, and in Belgrade by the Regent of Yugoslavia. Diplomatic reports from the capitals they visited show that the tour was generally considered to have extended British influence. The British Ambassador in Athens, after describing the excellent diplomatic effect of the King's visit, also commented that he had found him 'almost a case of arrested development', suffering from

Scenes from the *Nahlin* cruise. Group photo (left to right): the King, Wallis, Katherine Rogers, the King's Assistant Private Secretary Captain Alan Lascelles, and the King's equerry Sir John Aird.

A cigarette case given
by Wallis to the King
for Christmas 1935,
decorated with a map
of their holidays, the
places they had visited
set in diamonds. The
route of the 1936 holi-
day was added later.

'an unsatisfied craving for domesticity' to which Mrs Simpson seemed to represent 'a serious response'. He wondered 'whether this union, however queer . . . and embarrassing for the state, may not in the long run turn out to be more in harmony with the spirit of the age than anything that wisdom could have contrived'.

After they had spent a few days at Vienna, the King returned to England by air from Zurich, while Wallis went on to Paris, staying at the Hôtel Meurice. She began to suffer from a cold, and took to her bed. While she was languishing, she received her post, which contained letters from anxious friends, including her aunt, enclosing sensational American newspaper cuttings relating to both the holiday and her forthcoming divorce case. She was 'amazed and shocked'. Her friendship with the King and his intentions towards her had become 'a topic of dinner table conversation for every newspaper reader in the United States, Europe and the Dominions'. For Wallis, this was the turning point at which she woke up from her long fairy tale and began to visualize the catastrophe ahead. On 16 September, from her hotel bed, she wrote a drastic letter to the King breaking off their affair and saying she wished to return to Ernest Simpson, who had apparently got in touch with her offering to take her back.

> This is a difficult letter to write. . . . I must really return to Ernest. . . . I feel I am better with him than with you. . . . I am sure dear David that in a few months your life will run again as it did before and without my nagging. Also you have been independent of affection all your life. We have had lovely beautiful times together and I thank God for them and know that you will go on with your job doing it better and in a more dignified fashion each year. . . . I am sure you and I would only create disaster together. I shall always read all about you – believing only half! – and you will know I want you to be happy. I feel sure I can't make you so and I honestly don't think you can me. I shall have Allen [the King's solicitor] arrange the return of everything [the money he had settled on her]. I am sure that after this letter you will realize that no human being could assume this responsibility and it would be most unfair to make things harder for me by seeing me.

The King's reply to this eloquent plea for release was a letter beginning with the immortal line: 'Why do you say such hard things to David?' He felt 'hurt' and 'terribly unhappy' and 'bursting with love and such longing to hold you tighter than I ever have before'. Their separation – 'every moment of it' – was unendurable to him. He was dismayed at the thought of leaving for Balmoral without her – 'and not knowing when you are going to join me there'. According to the King's Assistant Private Secretary Alan Lascelles, the King threatened to cut his throat if she would not come to Scotland. Faced with such pressure, Wallis succumbed, and arrived in Aberdeenshire, accompanied by her friends the Rogers, on 23 September. With typical thoughtlessness, the King drove in person to meet her train at Ballater station, though he had declined to open a new hospital in Aberdeen that day, a duty that had been undertaken instead by the Duke and Duchess of York.

So began a nightmare autumn for Wallis. On the one hand she wanted to give up her divorce proceedings and go away, disappearing, at least temporarily, from the King's life. But the King would not hear of her leaving him; he threatened to follow her or to commit suicide; and she was too fond of him simply to ignore these threats and abandon him. He continued to shower her with magnificent jewellery, assuring her that he would be able to deal with any complications arising from the divorce. In fact, it is probable that he knew all along that abdication would be the price of his marriage project – he had already thought of giving up his rights to the throne a year earlier to pursue it – but he gave no hint of this to Wallis, his overwhelming concern being to reassure her and make her go along with his plans. Nothing seemed to matter to him but the pursuit of his heart's desire.

Soon after her return from Scotland at the beginning of October, Wallis went to live in a rented house at Felixstowe on the Suffolk coast: for her divorce was due to be heard at Ipswich at the end of the month (the London court lists being full), and she required a Suffolk residence. Her isolation there increased her anxiety. 'Do you still want me to go ahead', she wrote to the King on 14 October, 'as I feel it will hurt your popularity in the country?' Her own instincts were 'to steal quietly away'. She feared that 'you will have trouble in the House of Commons etc. and may be forced to go. I can't put you in that position.' The King, however, airily dismissed these fears. 'I know it sounds easy to say don't worry, but don't too much please Wallis. I'm doing half the

The King spent the second half of September entertaining a party at Balmoral, where he was joined on the 23rd by a reluctant Wallis, who had just tried unsuccessfully to end their relationship. He broke with tradition in that he did not invite senior figures of Government and Church, but his guests were scarcely disreputable, eight out of the sixteen being dukes or duchesses.

Left With the Duchess of Buccleuch.

Below (left to right) The King, Lord Louis Mountbatten, Kitty Rogers, Gladys Buist, Wallis, Edwina Mountbatten.

In her memoirs, Wallis claimed to have enjoyed her stay; but she must have felt out of place in such traditional surroundings, and her presence jarred on some of those present. She seems to have undertaken some functions of a hostess, as she had become used to doing at the Fort, and is said to have been snubbed by the Duchess of York when she came to dine with her husband.

Above With Kitty Rogers. *Below* Wallis, valliantly attempting to look like a countrywoman, walking on the hills with Slipper.

worrying and looking after things this end. . . . God bless WE my beloved sweetheart.' By 'looking after things', the King meant that he was in touch with her lawyers to ensure that the case went smoothly, with the newspaper owners to ensure that it received only the barest publicity in England, and with the Chief Constable of Suffolk to ensure that special measures were taken for her protection.

The twenty-seventh of October was the day of the hearing. Wallis had spent a sleepless night full of self-questionings. 'I paced the floor for hours, wondering whether I was doing the right thing. . . .' She arrived at the courthouse to find it surrounded by a mob of journalists, and had to be escorted inside by the police. The judge did not conceal his hostility to her, and she was nervous as she answered the few questions that her counsel, the celebrated Norman Birkett, was obliged to put to her. But after uncontested proceedings lasting nineteen minutes, she was awarded a decree *nisi* with costs. 'I suppose I must', said the judge reluctantly, 'in these unusual circumstances.' Wallis now faced an interval of six months before she could apply to have her divorce made absolute – during which interval political trouble was likely to arise as soon as the Government became aware of the King's desire to marry her. (It is interesting that she never seems to have considered applying for an annulment of her marriage to Ernest, which would have involved no waiting period, and to which she would presumably have been entitled if, as she is later said to have told Herman Rogers, the marriage had never been consummated.)

Wallis immediately returned to London, moving into a large furnished house in Cumberland Terrace, Regent's Park, which had been prepared for her in her absence. Here she would be able to live the life of an affluent society woman and entertain in style – but (as it happened) only for a month, during which she would be given little peace. That evening the King dined with her at her new residence and presented her with a magnificent emerald ring, inscribed with the words *WE are ours now, 27.x.36*: this was intended as her engagement ring. (The stone did not, as was later rumoured, come from the collection of Queen Alexandra, but had been found by Cartier.) The King also mentioned to her that, a week earlier, the Prime Minister had come to see him at the Fort to express concern about the divorce: this greatly alarmed her, but he assured her that he would be able to 'fix' everything.

It was indeed a great day for the King for, by going through with her divorce

Two pictures taken at the rented house at Felixtowe where Wallis spent two nervous weeks while awaiting her divorce hearing at Ipswich. *Above* The King, who visited her whenever he could and tried to sustain her morale. *Below* Wallis's best English friends, the kindly George and Kitty Hunter, who kept her company during the difficult days and tried to warn her of the dangerous consequences her divorce might have for the King.

Wallis's platinum and emerald engagement ring, made by Cartier and presented to her by the King after she had reluctantly gone through with her divorce case. Jacques Cartier told Marie Belloc Lowndes that the emerald came from an immense stone 'as large as a bird's egg' which had once belonged to the Grand Mogul, and had been divided up as there was thought to be no-one in the world extravagant enough to buy the whole of it.

in spite of her misgivings, Wallis had burnt her boats, and he could be confident that she was now his for the future. Having previously been irritable and unpunctual, he was now in excellent spirits: during his remaining six weeks on the throne, he performed his duties well and was charming to everyone. But there were few who shared his sense of relief, for the divorce gave rise to intense speculation as to whether he intended to marry Wallis. Diaries of the period show that little else was discussed in London's grander drawing rooms during the first days of November – and there was already talk both of abdication and the possibility of a morganatic solution. Such discussion was still largely confined to official and high society circles, for the British press continued to remain discreetly silent about Wallis. But such silence could not continue indefinitely, for the girl from Baltimore who might soon become Queen of England was a leading news item in the American press, and it could not be long before news of 'the King's matter' burst upon an astonished British public.

On 3 November, dressed as an admiral, and looking 'graceful, slender and handsome', the King performed the traditional ceremony of the State Opening of Parliament. By custom Lady Londonderry, one of the great London hostesses, gave a reception after this event at her palatial house in Park Lane, and the King attended this, accompanied by Wallis. A few days later Lady Londonderry met Wallis and told her that her association with the King threatened to damage the throne. Wallis wrote to her: 'I have been thinking over all you told me last night. I have come to the conclusion that perhaps no-one has been *really* frank with a certain person in telling him how the country feels about his friendship with me . . . and therefore I am going to tell him the things you told me.' Another noted hostess, Sibyl Colefax, who stayed at the Fort during the week-end of 7 November (which would turn out to be the last social party there), found Wallis

> really miserable. All sorts of people had come to her reminding her of her duty and begging her to leave the country. 'They do not understand', she said, 'that if I did so, the King would come after me regardless of anything. They would then get their scandal in a far worse form than they are getting it now.'

The King attending the Armistice Day ceremony on 11 November 1936, with his mother (opposite) and his brothers the Dukes of York and Kent (above). Two days earlier, he had told Walter Monckton of his determination to marry Wallis, even at the cost of his throne; and within a week, he would make the same announcement to the Prime Minister and to his family.

Again Wallis remonstrated with the King but, as before, he was beyond reason and refused to hear of her leaving. Indeed, on 9 November he confessed to Walter Monckton, his old friend and trusted adviser, that he was determined to marry her as soon as she was free, come what may.

On 11 November the King presided at the Armistice Day commemorations, and the following day he left on an inspection tour of the Home Fleet at Portland. This was a triumph. 'Here indeed was the Prince Charming who could win the hearts of all sorts and conditions of men and send a thrill through great crowds', recalled the First Lord of the Admiralty, Sir Samuel Hoare, who accompanied the King. 'When I travelled back with him, I was amazed at his liveliness after two days of continuous inspections in the worst possible weather.' On the evening of Friday 13 November the King returned to

In mid-November 1936, Aunt Bessie arrived from America to join Wallis in her hour of crisis. At the Fort, they were photographed together by the King, who appears in shadow on the bottom left of the picture.

the Fort, where Wallis was awaiting him along with Aunt Bessie, who had joined her niece in England during her difficult hour.

There also awaited him a letter from his Private Secretary, Major Hardinge, a somewhat cold personality who, since his appointment four months earlier, had not enjoyed a good relationship with his master. This made two points: that 'the silence of the British press on the subject of Your Majesty's friendship with Mrs Simpson' was about to be broken, with potentially 'calamitous' results; and that the cabinet was meeting 'to discuss the serious situation which is developing'. (Neither statement was in fact quite true.) Hardinge concluded that there was 'only one step' that could avert a political crisis, 'and that is for Mrs Simpson to go abroad *without further delay*'. The King claimed in his memoirs to have been angered by this letter, though it cannot have told him much that he did not already know or suspect. He did not at first show it to Wallis, but discussed it on Sunday 15 November with the trusted Walter Monckton, to whom he finally said: 'The first thing I must do is to send for the

Prime Minister. I shall tell him that if, as would now appear, he and the Government are against my marrying Mrs Simpson, I am prepared to go.'

When later that day the King showed Hardinge's letter to Wallis, she was stunned. She felt the only thing to do was to take Hardinge's advice and leave the country, as she had wanted for some time to do anyway. 'Summoning all the powers of persuasion in my possession', she wrote in her memoirs, 'I tried to convince him of the hopelessness of our position. For him to go on hoping, to go on fighting the inevitable, could only mean tragedy for him and catastrophe for me.' The King however would not listen. Taking her hand, he told her calmly: 'I'm going to send for Mr Baldwin to see me at the Palace tomorrow. I'm going to tell him that if the country won't approve our marrying, I'm ready to go.' Wallis burst into tears.

The King duly summoned Baldwin and, on the night of Monday 16 November, told him that marriage to Wallis had become 'an indispensable condition to my continued existence, whether as a King or a man. If I could marry her as King, well and good; I would be happy and in consequence a better King. But if, on the other hand, the country opposed the marriage, *then I was prepared to go*'. He then informed his mother and three brothers of his decision: all were horrified. The Duke of York, who would succeed to the throne on the King's abdication, was struck dumb by the news, though shortly afterwards both he and the Duchess wrote to the King to assure him they wanted him to be happy 'with the one person you adore'. The King also discussed his decision with two cabinet ministers who were personal friends of his, Sam Hoare and Duff Cooper, neither of whom held out much hope that the Government would sanction the marriage. Like many others during the coming days, Cooper suggested the King shelve the marriage question until after his Coronation, but this he refused to do, saying that it would amount to 'being crowned with a lie on my lips'. Following these meetings, the King departed on the night of 17 November on what was to be his last royal tour, a two-day visit to the depressed region of South Wales, during which he uttered the celebrated remark that 'something must be done' about unemployment.

Fifteen years later, when the Duke of Windsor wrote his memoirs, he implied that a struggle began at this point between himself and the Government over the marriage question. In fact, a careful study of the sources suggests that, when he saw his ministers and relations on 16–17 November, it was already his firm intention to abdicate, an intention which he never seriously reconsidered during the three weeks that followed. However, Wallis, who was aghast at the idea of his abdicating, pressed him to look for some compromise which might enable him to stay on his throne. To please her, the King went through the motions of examining these alternatives, though the evidence suggests that he never seriously pursued them or believed in them.

The first such idea which she put to him was that of trying to secure a morganatic marriage – that is, a union of a type known to continental monarchies in which a wife 'of lesser birth' does not share the titles or dignities of her royal husband. This had been suggested to Wallis by her friend Esmond Harmsworth, heir to the newspaper owner Lord Rothermere, though the original inspiration was probably Winston Churchill's. The King knew all about such things, as his own mother was the grandchild of a morganatic union: knowing of the embarrassment she had suffered as a child as a result of her semi-royal status, he regarded the notion with distaste. Nevertheless, when Wallis put it to him on his return from South Wales, he agreed to pursue it. On 25 November he summoned Baldwin again and asked him to ascertain whether the British and Dominion Governments would be willing to introduce legislation allowing him to marry morganatically. In fact, he had few illusions as to what the answer would be; and his enquiries (as Lord Beaverbrook warned him) were likely to accelerate his departure by inviting his governments at home and abroad to tender binding advice on the marriage question. The fact that he asked the sceptical Baldwin to consult the Dominion Governments, whereas the King was constitutionally entitled to do so himself through his Governors-General, is strong evidence that he did not look upon the morganatic marriage as a serious alternative to abdication.

During these days the King and Wallis appeared in London society together for the last time. Those who saw them, and knew something of what was happening, were amazed at his euphoria and her calmness. At a dinner party given by Chips Channon on 18 November the King was 'in a gay mood . . . nothing could mar his excellent temper as we went in to dinner'. He even joked to Duff Cooper about his coming abdication – 'it will be the last thing I do before I go'. Wallis's neighbour noticed that 'every few minutes he gazes at her and a happiness and radiance fills his countenance such as makes you have a lump in your throat'. The following day Cecil Beaton visited Wallis at Cumberland Terrace to show her the proofs of some recent photographs he had taken of her, and found her 'immaculate, soignée and fresh as a young girl', speaking 'in staccato sentences punctuated by explosive bursts of laughter that lit up her face with great gaiety'. They were joined by the King, who was delighted by the pictures and asked for copies of every one. He was 'in bright spirits' and full of jokes; when Wallis finally announced that they must all leave, he was 'like a child whose before-dinner play hour had come to an end'. On 26 November, when Chips Channon met her dining with Lady Stanley, he found her 'charming, sweet and gay', though reserved and unwilling to talk about the future.

The Stanley party, as it happened, was to be the last Wallis attended in London for many years. Life was becoming impossible for her in London, with a constant throng of curious or hostile strangers outside her door. 'All classes now know about the affair', wrote Marie Belloc Lowndes, 'and Mrs Simpson receives by every post frightful letters from religious lunatics threatening to kill her. She is closely guarded, and goes practically nowhere.' On Friday 27 November the King suggested that she and Aunt Bessie should leave London and retreat to the Fort with its privacy and security. No doubt the King had an ulterior motive: he knew that many of the people she was seeing in London were trying to get Wallis to leave him, and he wanted to remove her from their influence.

However, soon after she had installed herself at the Fort, Wallis finally decided that she must now do what she had meant to do since mid-September, and disappear from England and the King's life as soon as possible. As she confided to Sibyl Colefax in a letter of 30 November:

> I am planning quite by myself to go away for a while. I think everyone would like that – except one person perhaps – but I am planning a clever means of escape. After a while my name will be forgotten by the people and only two people will suffer instead of the mass of people who aren't interested anyway in individual feelings but only the workings of a system. I have decided to risk the result of leaving [the effect on the King] because it is an uncomfortable feeling to be stopping in a house where the hostess has tired of you as a guest. . . .

And to 'Foxy' Gwynne, an American friend from Washington days who was soon to marry the King's friend Lord Sefton, she wrote that 'everything is wrong and going more wrong – and I am so tired of it all. . . . I think I shall remove myself . . . for a small trip and give it all time to die down – perhaps returning when that d——d crown has been firmly placed'.

But it was too late. The storm was about to break. On the evening of 2 December the King took Wallis aside after dinner at the Fort and told her two grave pieces of news which had come to him that day. First, the press were about to break silence, following a speech by the Bishop of Bradford referring to the King's 'need for divine guidance'. Secondly, the King had seen Baldwin again, who had informed him that neither the British nor Dominion Governments could support the morganatic marriage, and that he was consequently left with only three choices: giving up the marriage; marrying contrary to the advice of his ministers (who would resign); or abdication. Horrified, Wallis announced that she must leave the country next day; she also begged the King to broadcast to his people telling them that he was giving her up. The King agreed she should leave, as life would be impossible for her in England once the press had started to write about her, and he promised to discuss the question of a broadcast with the Prime Minister.

Wallis's chosen destination was the Villa Lou Viei at Cannes, where her old friends the Rogers, whom she had last seen at Balmoral, had offered her a refuge. It was in a state of confusion and trepidation that she prepared to set out there on Thursday 3 December, for the British newspapers that morning were full of the crisis resulting from the King's wish to marry her (though only one of them, the *Daily Mirror*, as yet carried a photograph of her and personal details about her). As her escort the King chose his friend and courtier Lord Brownlow (who, unbeknown to the King, was already involved in secret efforts to get her to renounce him in order to keep him on the throne). In the late afternoon Wallis and Brownlow drove off to catch the ferry at Newhaven, Wallis doubting whether she would ever see the King again. His parting words to her were: 'I will never give you up.' Before she sailed, however, she scribbled a last note to him, referring to the proposed broadcast: 'Be calm with B[aldwin] but tell the country I am lost to you. . . .'

The long journey was nightmarish. Brownlow lacked a sense of direction, and frequently got lost as they drove across Northern France. From various hotels Wallis, using a prearranged code, tried to telephone the King, begging him 'on no account to step down' and to 'do nothing rash', but the connections

In his abdication broadcast, Edward mentioned that 'the other person most nearly concerned has tried up to the last to persuade me to take a different course'. This is confirmed by Wallis's last letters to the King. On 3 December, about to sail for France, she asks him to 'tell the country [in a radio broadcast] I am lost to you. . . .' And three days later, having taken refuge with the Rogers at Cannes, she writes to him by air mail: 'I am so anxious for you not to *abdicate*. . . .'

were so bad that they could hardly hear each other. At Blois in Touraine they were horrified to discover a crowd of reporters and cameramen at the hotel where they spent Friday night; and though they managed to escape, after bribing a porter to smuggle them out by the staff entrance, the press caught up with them again at Lyon after a bystander had shouted: *'Voilà la dame!'* After further adventures, they finally arrived at Lou Viei in the early hours of Sunday morning, Wallis, to avoid the gaze of the waiting journalists, crouching in the

At the Villa Lou Viei (left to right): Lord Brownlow, Kitty Rogers, Wallis, Herman Rogers.

back of the car with a rug over her head. She was now under siege (as was the King at the Fort), but at least 'back among friends'.

When Wallis woke up the next morning (6 December), she was 'seized with a feeling of helplessness', and though she managed to have an audible telephone conversation with the King, she found him 'remote and unreachable'. She then wrote him an extraordinary letter, fifteen pages long and barely coherent, a testimony to her mood of desperation at that moment and aimed above all at getting him to stay his hand in the obstinate and unbalanced state in which he was. It began: 'I am so anxious for you not to *abdicate*. . . .' She pointed out (correctly) that she would be blamed for his departure 'because they will say that I could have prevented it'. She begged him (at Brownlow's suggestion) to offer to drop the idea of marriage at least until the following autumn. 'By October Mr B couldn't afford to say no and I think the Dominions could be won over. Think my sweetheart isn't it better in the long run not to be hasty or selfish but back up your people and make an eight month sacrifice for them? Then . . . no one can say that you . . . ran away when your people were rallying to your aid.' If he insisted on abdicating, she warned him to settle various questions in advance, such as her final divorce decree, the pension to which he would be entitled, and the future titles they would both carry – 'all those 3 things must be bound up impossible to find a flaw'. (This, as it turned out, was prudent advice, though the King had managed to settle none of these matters by the time he abdicated.)

Meanwhile, the King was doing little to save his throne. He had been in touch with various people who had offered to support him, such as Winston Churchill and Lord Beaverbrook, but finally had told them all that he did not want their support, and had withdrawn to the Fort to put himself beyond their reach. He had asked Baldwin if he might broadcast – not, as Wallis wished, to announce that he was giving her up, but to plead in favour of a morganatic marriage – and not surprisingly had been turned down. Finally, he had asked only for legislation to make Wallis's divorce absolute immediately, so that he could join and marry her as soon as he abdicated; and though Baldwin was personally in favour of this, it was rejected by the cabinet when it met that Sunday. Even this disappointment could not deflect the King from his final decision, which he communicated to his brother the Duke of York on the Monday and to the Government on the Tuesday.

At Cannes, Brownlow, as he had promised his friends in London, set about getting Wallis to give up the King – only to discover that this was exactly what she herself wanted. Together they prepared a statement which they released to the press on Monday the 7th, stating that she wished 'to avoid any action or proposal which would hurt or damage His Majesty' and was willing 'to withdraw from a situation which has become both unhappy and untenable'. When this had no effect, the Government, in a final attempt to avert the Abdication, flew her divorce solicitor, Theodore Goddard, out to join her; and on Wednesday morning he rang Downing Street with the message that his client was willing 'to withdraw her petition for divorce and . . . do anything to prevent the King from abdicating', Goddard being satisfied that this represented her 'genuine and honest desire'. But it was too late; the King had now abdicated in all but name, and stood (if she gave up her divorce) to lose both his throne and the prospect of marrying her. Wallis even planned to leave for China with Brownlow, but the King assured her that he would still abdicate, and follow her wherever she went until he caught up with her.

The formalities of giving up the throne were quickly completed, the King, witnessed by his four brothers, signing an Instrument of Abdication at the Fort on the morning of Thursday 10 December, which became law on Friday afternoon. The Duke of York then became King George VI and announced his intention of creating his predecessor Duke of Windsor, by which name he was henceforth known (though the title was not formally created until March 1937). That night, after dining with his family at Windsor in an atmosphere of great sadness, the ex-King made his celebrated farewell broadcast, announcing to the world that he had found it 'impossible to do my duty as King and Emperor without the help and support of the woman I love', although he stressed that she had 'tried up to the last to persuade me to take a different course'. He then left for Austria, where the Rothschilds had offered him Schloss Enzesfeld, their castle near Vienna. Since informing Baldwin, twenty-five days earlier, that he was prepared to abdicate, he had done little to indicate that he wanted to remain King at all; and it has often been suggested that he wanted to give up his royal burden in any case, regarding Wallis, perhaps subconsciously, as a means of escape.

In the drawing room at Lou Viei, in the company of the Rogers and Lord Brownlow, Wallis listened to the broadcast lying on a sofa, covering her eyes

Accompanied by his faithful adviser Walter Monckton, the dazed ex-King heads for exile
after delivering his broadcast.

with her hands to hide her tears. Her worst nightmare had come to pass, and
the universe seemed to disintegrate around her. After the others had left her, 'I
lay there a long time before I could control myself enough to walk through the
house and go upstairs to my room'.

The Duke and Duchess of Windsor on their wedding day, 3 June 1937.

CHAPTER SIX

'The whole world against us and our love'

1936–37　　The Abdication was traumatic for Wallis. Never in her blackest moments had she imagined that her royal romance would end this way. In the eyes of the world, she was to blame for the King's departure; and to millions of people (particularly women) who had adored the departing King, she was a figure of hatred, a scheming adventuress who had ensnared him and diverted him from the path of duty. A torrent of hate mail descended on the Villa Lou Viei. As she wrote in her memoirs: 'To be accused of things one has never done, to be judged and condemned by people ignorant of the circumstances . . . such are the most corrosive of human experiences.' She survived only 'by mastering my emotions', and constantly assuring herself that she had done nothing wrong.

During the autumn her main thought had been to escape from the King; but now that, so much against her wishes, he had made his terrible sacrifice for her, her feelings towards him were loving and protective. It seemed tragic that they had to spend further months apart – for any reunion before her divorce became absolute (which could not happen before April) risked jeopardizing the proceedings. Her first letter to the new Duke of Windsor, written on 12 December 1936, the day he made his journey from England to Austria, contained no words of reproach.

Darling – My heart is so full of love for you and the agony of not being able to see you after all you have been through is pathetic. At the moment we have the whole world against us and our love. . . . I am feeling all your feelings of loneliness and despair which must face you on this new beginning. . . . I long for you so. . . . We must not take any risks because to have an accident now would be too much to bear – so please be a 'sissy' about protection. . . . I don't know your name but rather hoped it would be the

Prince [*sic*] of Windsor. . . . Your broadcast was very good my angel and it is all going to be so very lovely. . . . It is cruel the laws are such that we can't see each other till April. . . . I hope you will never regret this sacrifice and that your brother will prove to the world that we still have a position and that you will be given some jobs to do. I love you David and am holding so tight.

The Duke also found the prospect of such a long separation almost unbearable, but thought very little about what he had given up, or the practical difficulties he would now have to face. His mind was completely concentrated on the blissful prospect of reunion with and marriage to Wallis. In his first post-Abdication letter to her of 22 December, he looked forward to

. . . that dear sweet day when we will 'officially' belong to each other. Oh! Wallis, why must we wait so long? It's so cruel. But we . . . have been through so much for each other and for our perfect happiness that we can take this . . . as bravely as we have faced the World the last two months. It's all so lovely Wallis and so dear and sweet and sacred and I'm really happy for the very first time in my life. . . . We'll just have to write this Christmas off and make up for it by so many lovely happy ones in future. I will go to Church in Vienna on Friday . . . and pray so hard that God goes on blessing WE for the rest of our lives. He has been very good to WE and is watching over US I know. . . . I love you love you Wallis more and more and more and am holding so tight.

Such had been the Duke's obsession with Wallis, so eager had he been to cast off the crown once he realized he could not share it with her, that he had hardly stopped to think what life would be like for him after he had abdicated. With that boyish naïvety which never left him, he vaguely assumed that his family would give their blessing to his marriage and that, after an interval to give George VI a chance to settle in, they would welcome him back to England with his new wife. Wallis had no such illusions. As she wrote to him in the New Year: 'Naturally we have to build up a position but how hard it is going to be with no signs of support from your family. One realizes now the impossibility of getting marriage announced in the Court Circular and of the HRH. It is all a great pity. . . . To set off on our journey with proper backing would mean so much. . . .' She tried to wake the Duke up to the realities of his situation, and to get him to stand up for himself. 'Since you have been so trusting all along perhaps you are now beginning to realize that you can't go on being and then have praise after you are dead. . . . I should write your brother a straightforward letter setting forth the reasons for him not to treat you as an outcast . . . so that we have a dignified and correct position as befits an ex-King of England who really only left to get what the present one was lucky enough to have.' She understood, as he did not, the enormous adjustments he would now have to make. 'Your life has been led at such a great and busy pace that inactivity will be very trying for you my loved one.'

Wallis and the Duke had meant to stay only briefly at Lou Viei and Enzesfeld; but it was hard for them to move elsewhere without attracting public attention, their kind hosts urged them to stay on, and in the end they each remained in their respective refuges for more than three months. The Duke was able to lead a spacious existence in his luxurious Austrian castle, to go skiing and visit Vienna; but at Cannes, Wallis hardly dared leave the small confines of the villa – she was receiving daily death threats through the post, and could not even go shopping without attracting a crowd of gapers. The Rogers tried to keep up her morale; but it is hardly surprising that, with the passing weeks of claustophobia, frustration, threatening letters and hostile newspaper articles, Wallis's correspondence with the Duke assumed a slightly paranoid tone. Though she knew better than anyone that it was the King's own obstinacy that had led to his abdication, she wrote to him suggesting that he had been the victim of a plot by British politicians: 'I was the convenient tool in their hands and how they used it!' She blamed two people above all for the chill winds from the British Establishment. One was Baldwin: 'You cannot allow that man to finish you – and believe me, that is the idea!' The other was the new Queen consort. 'Really David, the pleased expression on the Duchess of York's [*sic*] face is funny to see', she wrote at the end of December. 'How she is loving it all. There will be no support there.' And again in February: 'I blame it all on the wife – who hates us both.'

What drove her particularly off-balance was an element of uncertainty over whether she would even obtain her final divorce decree, leaving the possibility that the Duke, having abdicated in order to marry her, might in the end be

Wallis at Cannes; the Duke of Windsor at Enzesfeld. They were forced to live apart for five months, and their letters expressed the pain of their separation.

is lovely to have 1936 behind us and only this and many more happy years together to look forward to – OR! WE will make it – this separation but "by golly" it is hard and a terrible strain – If it wasn't for that unsatisfactory telephone then I really would go mad – Oh! poor everybody WE all say and HE is so

SCHLOSS ENZESFELD

1st January 1937

Hello! my sweetheart. Such a very happy New Year I wish for WE from the fastness of my "exile" – my exile from you and not from England my darling and although it is still a matter of weary months to wait it unable to do so. For the authorities in England felt it necessary, through an official known as the King's Proctor, to investigate rumours that she and the Duke had been engaging in an adulterous affair: had evidence of adultery come to light, the divorce (under the laws of the time) would have failed. As we have suggested, it is improbable that an act of full sexual intercourse had taken place during the course of their relationship; but with so much hostility to their marriage, who could tell what such an investigation might produce? 'It is despair for me to be so badly treated', she wrote to the Duke in a rare moment of self-pity.

Despite the agony of uncertainty, Wallis, inveterate organizer that she was, began to make plans for their wedding, simply informing the Duke of her decisions. From the various houses that had been offered to them, she chose Candé, a modernized château in the Loire Valley owned by Charles Bedaux, the famous French-American time-and-motion tycoon, and his wife Fern, good friends of the Rogers. The Duke wanted to marry Wallis the moment she got her divorce in late April or early May, but she decided that it would be more fitting to wait until some time after the Coronation on 12 May. She then told the Duke to write to the King explaining these choices as if they had been his own, and requesting royal 'approval'. Even at a distance of almost a thousand miles, she took control of his life in the manner that he so enjoyed and had come to expect of her.

On 9 March Wallis and the Rogers left Lou Viei and made the long road journey to Candé, where they received a warm welcome from Fern Bedaux. It was bliss for Wallis to find herself in a large, comfortable and well-staffed country house (from which the owners tactfully withdrew, leaving her in charge) and to be able to amble in the spacious grounds. By the end of March the difficulties in the way of the divorce had come to an end, though the decree itself remained some weeks away, and until it was pronounced the Duke was advised that it would be dangerous even to be in the same country as his future wife. He did however send her Slipper, the Cairn terrier that he had given her in 1934, and who had kept him company since he had parted from Wallis at Fort Belvedere on 3 December 1936. However, while she was walking with this beloved dog at Candé on 6 April, he was bitten by a viper and died. She wrote to the Duke:

Already under stress after four months apart, Wallis and the Duke were overwhelmed by the sudden death of their dog Slipper.

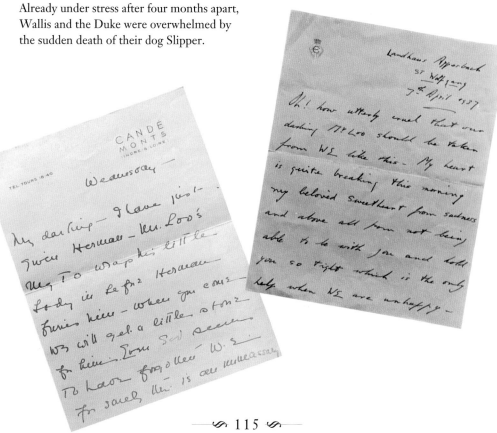

Even God seems to have forgotten WE for surely this is an unnecessary sorrow for us. He was our dog – not yours or mine but ours – and he loved us both so. Now the principal guest at the wedding is no more. I can't stop crying but we must be brave and suffer the next 3 weeks. . . . We are both feeling the strain – I can hear it in your beloved voice – that defeated sound. . . .

He replied:

Oh! how utterly cruel that our darling Mr Loo should be taken from WE like this. My heart is quite breaking this morning my beloved sweetheart from sadness and above all from not being able to be with you and hold

Reunited at Candé, May 1937.

you so tight which is the only help when WE are unhappy. . . . I feel quite stunned and dread the remaining three weeks until I am to be with you never to be parted ever again my sweetheart. . . .

Finally, on 3 May, Wallis's divorce became absolute; and the Duke of Windsor joined her at Candé from Austria the following day. He looked thin and drawn, but rushed up the steps to embrace her. They had been apart for five months. 'Before, we had been alone in the face of overwhelming trouble', Wallis wrote in her memoirs. 'Now we could meet it side by side.'

Trouble there certainly was; for it soon became apparent that their wedding – which was fixed for 3 June – would be boycotted by the Royal Family. Not only would none of the Duke's close relations be attending, but the King would not authorise any of his courtiers to be present, or any senior officials of the Crown. Not even old friends of the Duke of Windsor such as Lord Brownlow, who held a royal appointment as Lord-Lieutenant of Lincolnshire, or Lord Louis Mountbatten, whom he had asked to be his best man, dared to come. This came as no great surprise to Wallis, whose letters show that she well understood which way the wind was blowing, but was shattering to the Duke, who could hardly grasp why his family were taking such an attitude towards the event on account of which (and from honourable motives, as he saw it) he had given up the throne and which obviously meant everything to him.

A further blow was to come. On 27 May, a week before he was due to be married, the Duke received a letter from the King informing him that Letters Patent had been issued providing that his future wife would not be entitled to share his royal title or rank. 'This is a fine wedding present!' he exclaimed. 'I know Bertie – I know he couldn't have written this letter on his own. Why in God's name would they do this to me at this time!' The King's letter explained that he had been reluctantly obliged to take this step as a result of ministerial advice he had received. However, Philip Ziegler's official biography of Edward VIII makes clear that the British Government was unhappy about denying royal rank to the Duchess of Windsor, which it considered legally unjustified, and only issued its 'advice' after much hesitation and at the insistence of the King and his courtiers.

This act of discrimination was to rankle bitterly with the Duke for the rest

Comme en un roman d'autrefois
Cette Demeure noble et fière
abrita dans son cœur de pierre
la loyauté d'un cœur de roi.

Château de Candé - 3 Juin 1937

Above The Chateau de Candé.
Opposite A sapphire and diamond bracelet given to Wallis by the Duke in commemoration of their French marriage contract, 18 May 1937.

of his life. It amounted to a public condemnation of his marriage, an official pronouncement that his wife was not good enough for him. Moreover, the previous autumn, as King, he had been assured by the Government that it would be impossible for him to contract a morganatic marriage, whereas now that he had abdicated, he was being condemned to just such a morganatic union, unique in modern British history. Never would he reconcile himself to this situation, or forgive the act (which was of doubtful legality) purporting to deny his status to his wife. To Wallis the whole matter was less of a surprise (she had anticipated difficulties on this score even before the abdication) and of less importance. Her main concern was that their marriage should not lack dignity, and (as she put it in her memoirs) that she should not be seen as 'the woman who had come between David and his family'.

The marriage of the Duke of Windsor to Wallis Warfield (some weeks earlier she had resumed her maiden name by deed poll), conducted by a rogue vicar

Left The bride and groom.

Below Fern Bedaux, Katherine Rogers, Lady Alexandra Metcalfe, Aunt Bessie, Dudley Forwood, the Duke, Fruity Metcalfe and Herman Rogers.

Opposite above Herman Rogers (having given away the bride), Dudley Forwood (the Duke's equerry), Randolph Churchill and Wallis.

Opposite below left Wallis with Walter Monckton.

Opposite below right The Duke and Duchess with the best man, Fruity Metcalfe.

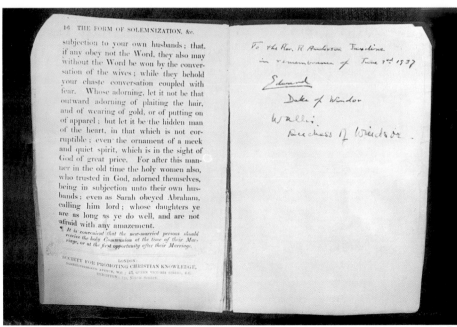

from the North of England, Dr Jardine, who was acting in defiance of his bishop, took place in the music room at Candé, which had been converted into a chapel for the occasion, on 3 June 1937. No relations of the Duke were present, nor any British official apart from the Consul at Tours. Herman Rogers gave Wallis away, and the Duke's old boon companion Fruity Metcalfe acted as best man. The sprinkling of other guests included Aunt Bessie, Walter Monckton, the Bedaux, the Rothschilds, Randolph Churchill, Lady Diana Cooper and the wife of the British Ambassador to Vienna. The event represented the ultimate fulfilment of the Duke's desire, but during the six months since he had abdicated, he had developed feelings of bitter resentment against his family in England and indeed the whole British official establishment, who had made it clear by their behaviour that they regarded him and his fiancée as outcasts. As for the new Duchess of Windsor, she wrote in her memoirs that it was for her 'a supremely happy moment'; but she must have known that the married life ahead would not be a bed of roses. Though the Duke would remain utterly devoted to her to his dying day, she knew she would have to work hard to satisfy a man who had once been busy, but now had little to do; who had once been supremely important, and was now a has-been; who had once been surrounded by people who organized every practical aspect of his existence, but now relied on her as his chief of staff; whose dream was to be with her every moment of every day, to rely on her every word and satisfy her every desire; whom in one sense she regarded as the *beau idéal* of an English gentleman, in another, a charming but petulant little boy.

Opposite above The music room at Candé, where the marriage service took place on 3 June 1937.

Opposite below The marriage service sheet inscribed by the newly-weds for the Anglican vicar, the Reverend R. Anderson Jardine, who had defied his bishop to marry them.

Portrait drawing by Drian, used by the Windsors on their 1937 Christmas card.

CHAPTER SEVEN

'I think I can make him happy'

1937–39   As a married man, the Duke of Windsor always reacted indignantly to the suggestion that his wife had been his mistress before their marriage. Few took his protestations seriously; yet as we have seen, it is possible that they did not enjoy full sexual relations before or indeed during their marriage and that the Duchess was not really capable of such acts. However, in the days before their wedding, the Windsors did address their minds to the possibility of having children: they would have liked, if the difficulties could be overcome, to seal their union and enrich their family life in this way. He was then about to be forty-three and she forty-one. They consulted a gynaecologist recommended by the Bedaux, who had themselves tried unsuccessfully to have children. The examination however confirmed the fact of the Duchess's incurable sterility. Having received this disappointing news, they put the question out of their minds, except that they briefly considered adopting a child in the 1950s, only to decide that it would be too complicated at their time of life (they were approaching sixty).

Children would undoubtedly have made a difference to their life and given it an added sense of purpose; it would also have been embarrassing for the Royal Family in England to have to deal with what would have been in effect a new Jacobite line. Documents executed at the time of the Abdication illustrate the concern of courtiers at the possibility that the departing monarch might have issue by his coming marriage: under Scots law (which had not abolished the concept of entail as English law had done in 1925), his son might have had a claim to the Balmoral Estate, and as part of the financial settlement resulting from the Abdication, the Duke was required to guarantee against this eventuality. In addition, the Letters Patent of 27 May 1937 purported to provide that any future children of the Duke of Windsor, as well as of his wife, should be denied the right to share his royal rank.

On their honeymoon in Venice and in Carinthia.

Stopping briefly at Venice, where they were mobbed by delighted crowds, the newly married Windsors made their way to Schloss Wasserleonburg, Count Munster's fairy-tale castle at Carinthia in Austria, where they were to spend their honeymoon. Like most arrangements of their married life, this had been fixed up by the Duchess, in correspondence with her friend Chips Channon who was a friend of the English Countess. There they spent three idyllic months recuperating from the stresses and strains of their recent adventures. 'The situation of the house is ideal and the country lovely', the Duchess wrote to her aunt, 'the house itself rather run down with a combination of Austrian and English comfort. . . . We have decided to treat it as a picnic and not worry until we recover from the last six months.'

At Wasserleonburg, it was inevitable that the Windsors should have given some thought to the dramatic events of the previous year, and discussed how things might have happened differently; but after a few fruitless talks of this kind, they sensibly agreed never to raise the subject again. But there were issues arising from the Abdication that continued to bear on their future; and the Duke spent much of the summer anxiously consulting his advisers about two matters. The first was the question of his and the Duchess's titles. The second concerned King George VI's reluctance to honour an agreement under which, in return for the Duke giving up all he had inherited on his father's death (notably his interest in the Sandringham and Balmoral estates), he would be guaranteed an annual pension of £25,000. On the matter of the title, the Duke, having obtained a legal opinion confirming the doubtful validity of the Letters Patent, wanted to make a grand gesture by renouncing his own royal title, thus reducing himself to the same status as his wife; but he changed his mind on her advice. The money question was more pressing, as the Windsors were unable to decide on what scale they were going to live until they knew what their income was likely to be; by the end of the summer, however, no word had yet come that the King intended to honour his promise.

On leaving Wasserleonburg in September, the Windsors were invited to join the Bedaux, their former hosts at Candé, at a hunting lodge in Hungary. 'This is a dirty house full of bugs and mosquitoes', wrote the Duchess to her aunt, 'but the shooting has been good and a wonderful sight to see the cowboys in their quaint costumes.' At Candé, Bedaux had flattered the Duke by suggesting that he might play some role as a world statesman, promoting international understanding and peace; and he now offered, through his international business empire, to organize a study tour of industrial conditions, first in Hitler's Germany in the latter part of October, then in Roosevelt's America during November and December. The Duke agreed to this with remarkably little thought and without consulting anyone. He had nothing much else to do; he was susceptible to Bedaux's persuasiveness; he was personally curious to visit both countries; and he wanted to give the Duchess something of a royal progress at the outset of their marriage. (In the view of the Duke's equerry Dudley Forwood, the last reason was the dominant one in the Duke's mind.) Afterwards, the Duke would feel that Bedaux had tried to exploit him from business motives; but this was not entirely fair, and in truth he had been unwise to agree to such high-profile tours within a year of giving up the throne, in view of his sensitive position as an ex-King and the intense publicity that always attended his and the Duchess's doings.

Unwise it may have been, but there was nothing particularly sinister in the Duke's decision to visit Nazi Germany with his wife in the autumn of 1937, before the full horror of that regime and its warlike intentions became known. It is true that, like much of the English ruling class, he was mildly fascinated by Hitler, admired his anti-communism, and felt the democracies ought to make some effort to satisfy German 'grievances' in order to avert the nightmare of another war. But it was by no means unusual at that time – the high noon of Appeasement – for eminent Englishmen to go to Germany and privately meet the Nazi dictator, as Lloyd George had done a year before, and Lord Halifax would do the following month. After the war, it transpired that Ribbentrop, Hitler's fatuous diplomatic adviser, had persuaded the Führer that the Duke had lost his throne mainly on account of friendship towards Nazi Germany, and might be susceptible to the idea of regaining it with German assistance. There is no evidence to support this fantastic theory, nor the suggestion that the Duchess, who had hardly a political thought in her head, admired the Nazis and influenced her husband in their favour, though no doubt she was as intrigued as he was to have a glimpse of that curious revolutionary regime.

In the event, the tour, lasting from 11 to 23 October, did not prove a wholly comfortable experience for the Windsors. In the company of their self-appointed host, Dr Ley of the Nazi labour organization the *Arbeitsfront*, a chronic and odious drunk, they were raced around the country, at a motoring speed which

In Germany, October 1937.
Inspecting a factory; with
their guide, the bibulous Dr
Ley, and other members of
the Nazi Labour Front; with
Hitler at Berchtesgaden.

terrified the Duchess, on an exhausting programme of visits to industrial and housing developments. The trip was given no official character in Germany and was reported without comment in the German press; but they were eagerly entertained by Goebbels, Goering, Hess and Ribbentrop. The Duchess wrote in her memoirs that the Nazi leaders both fascinated and repelled her; she wrote to her aunt from Leipzig that the trip was 'interesting . . . but very strenuous, so many things in a day and miles of walking through factories, housing settlements etc'. At the end of their trip they had tea with Hitler at Berchtesgaden. The interpreter Paul Schmidt later wrote that the Führer 'was evidently making an effort to be as amiable as possible towards the Duke, whom he regarded as Germany's friend', but that there was 'nothing whatever to indicate whether the Duke of Windsor really sympathized with the ideology and practices of the Third Reich, as Hitler seemed to assume he did'. Hitler later remarked to his entourage that the Duchess 'would have made a good Queen'. The Duchess for her part was fascinated by Hitler's fanatical piercing eyes, which reminded her of the only other dictator she had met, Atatürk, and had the impression that the Führer 'did not care for women'.

The Duchess undoubtedly relished the attention she received but saw such trips above all as something that might keep her husband interested and busy. What she most looked forward to was the planned tour of her native United States in November, where she had not been since 1933. Although their trip (like the German one) was said to be unofficial, the President had invited them to the White House, Mrs Roosevelt had offered to take them personally to see housing projects in which she was interested, and the United States Government was proposing to treat them with all the honour due to visiting foreign dignitaries – much to the embarrassment of the British Embassy in Washington which had been instructed virtually to ignore them. However, all arrangements were in the hands of Bedaux; and just as the Windsors were about to embark for America, he suddenly called the tour off, having become involved in disastrous quarrels both with his own business associates and the American labour unions. The Windsors were bitterly disappointed, but drew the wise lesson that there was little they could do for the time being in the public sphere without attracting unfavourable publicity.

For the moment, it merely remained for them to settle down into private life abroad until such time as they might return to live in England; but there was a problem in that George VI still showed himself reluctant to pay his brother the promised annuity of £25,000 in return for his having renounced his inheritance. Instead, he proposed to allow the lesser sum of £21,000 on condition that the Duke agreed never to return to England except by the consent of the authorities. The Duke wrote indignantly to the Prime Minister, Neville Chamberlain, that he regarded this proposal 'as both unfair and intolerable, as it would be tantamount to my accepting payment for remaining in exile'. Only in February 1938 was an arrangement of sorts reached, whereby the Duke began to receive his (reduced) allowance in return for 'taking note' of an official memorandum stating that, in the improbable event of his coming to England against the advice of the Government, the latter might have to advise the King to suspend any payments to his brother.

The Windsors imagined they would be returning to live in England after a few years, and until that time they decided to continue residing in France. Although they never mastered the language (the Duchess spoke it better than the Duke), they were given a hospitable welcome by that country, where they were granted immunity from taxation and their privacy was protected. The Duchess also adored the elegance of Paris. Until February 1938 they lived at the Hôtel Meurice, the most discreet of the great Parisian hotels: knowing they were an excellent advertisement for that establishment, the Duchess negotiated a rate of $30 a day for a magnificent private suite facing the Tuileries, an office, and board and lodging for their entire domestic and secretarial staff. In February 1938 they moved for three months to a furnished villa at Versailles, becoming neighbours of Sir Charles and Lady Mendl, a British diplomat and his remarkable American decorator wife who were their closest friends in France. In May 1938 they took a long lease of La Cröe, a large shorefront villa at Antibes on the Côte d'Azur, and they spent that summer supervising its decoration and filling it with the Duke's possessions from England. In October 1938, after a long search, the Duchess found a Paris town house suitable for formal entertaining in the Boulevard Suchet, and the next six months were mostly spent decorating and furnishing this property: it too was rented, for the Windsors (to their subsequent regret) did not wish to buy a house in which they believed they would not be living for long.

After the Windsor wedding Walter Monckton had warned the Duchess that the British people would not forgive her if she failed to make the Duke happy.

Above La Cröe.

Below The house in the Boulevard Suchet.

She replied to him: 'Walter, don't you think I have thought of all that? I think I can make him happy.' There can be no doubt that the Duke was blissfully happy throughout their marriage, that he always felt his decision (for all its unforeseen and dismaying consequences) to have been worthwhile, and that he never ceased to delight in her company or regard her as a most wonderful human being. Friends who saw him after his marriage found him looking infinitely happier and healthier than at any time during the previous few years: gone were the nervous movements and the black eye pouches, the signs of strain and fatigue. The Duchess for her part saw it as her duty to make his domestic life as comfortable as possible after all he had given up for her. She therefore did her best to look after him in the manner he enjoyed, protecting him, spoiling and chiding him, making sure he had everything he wanted and that he was always kept busy. She also sought to ensure that his surroundings were such as befitted the former King of England. In this latter respect, as she supervised the installation and administration of their two rented houses in France, she proved herself a considerable artist, noted for her imagination, perfectionism and organizing ability.

In decorating her houses, the Duchess had the advice of her friend Elsie Mendl, and employed the talents of Stéphane Boudin of Maison Jansen, who was famous for his ability to achieve theatrical period effects. But she had her own definite ideas of what she wanted, and was never satisfied until she had achieved exactly the effect she had in mind. She was extraordinarily quick to learn about the styles and furniture of the various periods, and techniques such as *trompe l'oeil*. She would supervise the work in progress like a general directing her troops. La Cröe was a huge and rather ugly villa in gleaming white: it reminded the Duchess rather of an ocean liner, and this was her theme in doing it up. The reception rooms were decorated in white and gold, with huge mirrors to make them look enormous; the Duke's sitting room at the top of the house was in the style of a captain's cabin, with mahogany and brass and a telescope looking out to sea; the terrace had a deck-like air. The Paris house had a false Louis XVI façade, and within it the Duchess (guided by Boudin) experimented with eighteenth-century furniture and styles. Miss Hood, who became the Duke's secretary at the time they took the lease on the Boulevard Suchet, recalled how the Duchess 'tirelessly searched for exactly the right furniture, rugs, materials, lamps and bibelots' and 'spent long hours in antique shops hunting for exactly the pieces she needed. No time or trouble seemed too much.' She would ask for a room to be redone if its decoration did not completely satisfy her, and spend whole days surrounded by crates of furniture and other wares sent on approval from *antiquaires*, arranging them in different ways. The house was finished to her exacting standards just in time for the start of the Paris season in May 1939, during which they entertained Paris society on a large scale for the first time.

The Duke had always had comptrollers and housekeepers to organize his servants and attend to the running of his houses, and these duties were now undertaken by the Duchess. With the exception of the Austrian valet and chauffeur who had accompanied the Duke to France in 1937, it was she who hired their staff, fixed their terms of employment, and instructed them in their duties, always insisting on the highest standards. By the summer of 1939 she had put together an excellent domestic staff of about thirty, headed by an outstanding English butler and French chef. Every morning the Duchess would discuss the daily menus with her chef, specifying not only the dishes she wanted but how she wished the food to be arranged aesthetically on the plate. She also insisted on personally scrutinizing almost every household bill before it was paid, instructing the secretaries (three Englishwomen) to prepare elaborate accounts which enabled her to keep track of expenditure from month to month. When the Windsors spent Christmas of 1938 at La Cröe with a party of friends, the Duchess personally attended to every arrangement, making sure all was in order for the comfort of her guests, choosing the tree, buying and wrapping dozens of presents, hiring extra staff, and organizing local entertainers to come and perform at the house.

The Duchess took care to consult the Duke before making any important decision or purchase, and he often had views to express, particularly regarding such matters as the arrangement of furniture. On the whole, however, he was delighted for her to be exclusively in charge of all domestic matters. When not playing golf, walking their dogs (three much-pampered cairn terriers) or receiving friends, the Duke was generally dealing with the enormous business correspondence, much of it acrimonious, that resulted from the Abdication. When he worked, he often spread his papers on the floor; this annoyed the Duchess, who hated any sort of unsightly disorder, and if she entered the room she would give him a look which would reduce him to a state of abject apology.

The dining room at the Boulevard Suchet, an example of the Duchess's decorative skills. A contemporary described it as 'a richly colourful room with its coral and white chairs and curtains, its black and gold table, its mirrored shutters, quaintly painted sideboards and gay pieces of *saxe* porcelain. . . .' Lighting the candles is the English butler Hale: he was on loan from the Bedaux at Candé, where P. G. Wodehouse was a frequent guest and is said to have used him as the model for Jeeves.

The Windsors at home (above) and at Genoa with the Rogers in August 1938 (below).

She also told him off in strident terms if, for example, he happened to walk with his golf shoes on a polished wooden floor.

The Duchess had the old-fashioned American instinct that nothing must be left undone for the comfort of her guests. She aimed to ensure that everything they might want they should have, that everything they saw should be pleasing to the eye, that every implement and material should be of the best, and that the food and drink they ate should be exceptional. Before the war she employed at various times Dyot and Pinaudier, considered to be among the half-dozen top French chefs of the period: she experimented endlessly with elaborate cocktail snacks, and introduced original features into her meals such as a dish to be served between two main courses which looked like a strawberry ice but turned out to be made of tomatoes. She sought to be a work of art in herself, and was always exquisitely turned out; of course, she spent much time with hairdressers, masseurs and other practitioners who aided beauty. She kept herself extremely thin. She dressed beautifully, usually in clothes made by Mainbocher, whose creations were famous for their straight lines, their severity and their simplicity: with her slenderness, her flatness and her angularity, the Duchess suited them ideally.

With the exception of such episodes as their Christmas house party at La Cröe and the Paris season, the Windsors did not however lead a particularly active social life in the two years before the war. They were careful about whom they saw. They did not like having their activities reported in the newspapers. For the most part they led an intensely private, intensely domestic existence, often dining on their own and going out to a cinema.

Though he was supremely happy in his married life, there were two matters that preyed on the Duke's mind during 1938–39. The first was the question of when he and the Duchess might return to England: at the time of their marriage they intended to make at least a visit there before 1939. A gallup poll suggested that 61 per cent of the British people wanted the Windsors to return to Britain and only 16 per cent were against this. The King, however, dreaded his brother's return: an ambassador who visited him in the autumn of 1937 found that he did 'not yet feel safe on his throne' and was like 'the medieval monarch who has a hated rival claimant living in exile'. When Monckton visited Balmoral a year later, he found that the Prime Minister wanted the Duke to come home soon to 'take some of the royal functions off his brother's hands',

The Duchess dressed by Mainbocher, whose straight lines she so suited.

At a cinema première in Paris.

but that the Queen 'felt quite plainly that it was undesirable to give the Duke any effective sphere of work' since he was 'an attractive, vital creature' who might pose a threat to her husband 'who was less superficially endowed with the arts and graces that please'. There was also the vexed question of whether, when the Windsors returned, the Royal Family would receive the Duchess. The Government had nothing against the Duke's return but was embarrassed by the thought of its taking place in circumstances which made it clear that he was not on good terms with his family. The Duke was therefore repeatedly advised to postpone his homecoming – advice which he accepted unhappily, as he was now very homesick. 'When I say I return to England tomorrow', wrote Harold Nicolson after visiting him at La Cröe, 'his eye twitches in pain. . . .'

The Duke was also disturbed by the deterioration of the international situation and the drift to war. 'Something really must be done to prevent these monthly incidents of agression [*sic*] and consequent crises', he wrote to Aunt

The Windsors at Verdun in May 1939, before the Duke delivered his 'peace broadcast'.

Bessie in April 1939 after Mussolini's invasion of Albania had forced them to cancel a holiday, 'and I personally am convinced that the dictator powers can be made to behave themselves without war which is certain to destroy civilization.' On 10 May, following an invitation from the American NBC company, he made a world peace broadcast from Verdun. 'I speak simply as a soldier of the last war, whose most earnest prayer is that such a cruel and destructive madness shall never again overtake mankind. . . . The grave anxieties of the time compel me to raise my voice in expression of the universal longing to be delivered from the fears that beset us. . . .' This caused a brief sensation, and the Duke received thousands of grateful letters from all over the world; although the BBC refused to carry the broadcast, it was widely reported in the British press, where the Duke appeared as a leading news item for the last time until his death. Yet he was criticized for drawing attention to himself at a time when the King and Queen were on their way to visit the United States.

The Windsors were at La Cröe, giving their summer house party, when the Nazi-Soviet Pact was announced on 22 August 1939. Right to the end they did not want to believe that war would occur: this was particularly so with the Duchess, who could hardly bear to think that all her hard work of the past fifteen months, creating her two domestic masterpieces, would suddenly be ruined. The Duke sent telegrams to both Hitler and King Victor Emmanuel of Italy, begging them 'as a citizen of the world' not to plunge Europe into conflict; but Germany invaded Poland on 1 September, and two days later Britain and France were at war.

The Windsors at war, 1939: the Duchess in the uniform of the motorized section of the
French Red Cross; the Duke in the uniform of a major-general in the Welsh Guards.

CHAPTER EIGHT

'Can you fancy a family continuing a feud. . . ?'

1939–40 Though horrified by the outbreak of hostilities, the Windsors were relieved to think they would now be able to return to live in England and put the family quarrel behind them. After conferring with the Palace, the British Government offered the Duke the choice of two minor war jobs: Deputy Civil Defence Commissioner for Wales, or liaison officer with the British Military Mission in Paris. He was to come to London to discuss these with the authorities, at which time he assumed other aspects of their future would be resolved. In a cloak-and-dagger atmosphere, they made their way north from Antibes to Cherbourg. The Duchess wrote to her aunt from Vichy on 10 September: 'Naturally the Duke wishes to do all he can for the country – quite a different point of view to what they have done for him the last 3 years. I shall miss France where everyone has been more than kind.'

At Cherbourg they were met by the Duke's old friend and shipmate Lord Louis Mountbatten, commanding the destroyer HMS *Kelly*, and Randolph Churchill, representing his father Winston Churchill who was now First Lord of the Admiralty. The party crossed the Channel to Portsmouth, where something of a shock awaited them. Though there was a guard of honour (on Churchill's instructions), they found no representative of the Royal Family to meet them, nor even a message. Their reception committee consisted of Walter Monckton, their faithful adviser, and Lady Alexandra Metcalfe, wife of the Duke's best man 'Fruity' Metcalfe, at whose house in Sussex they were going to stay (for there had been no invitation for them to stay at any of the royal residences).

Next day the Duke went to London where he spent an hour with the King. It was only with difficulty that George VI had been persuaded to agree to this one short meeting, to which he had consented on condition that their wives were not present and that no controversial subjects were mentioned. The only matter of substance discussed was the Duke's war job: of the two that had been offered, he said he would prefer the civil defence post in Wales to the liaison post in France. The two brothers were not to meet again for six years, and the Duke received no invitation to meet any other member of his family.

The following day the Duke went to the War Office. The War Secretary, Leslie Hore-Belisha, one of the few cabinet ministers to have been sympathetic to him in 1936, explained that the Welsh offer had been withdrawn, and that there only remained to him the job in France. The Duke accepted this with good grace, but asked whether, before returning there, he and the Duchess might be allowed to visit the Home Commands. Hore-Belisha was confident of being able to secure this; but when he went to see the King about it, George VI was horrified. 'He thought that if the Duchess toured the commands, she might get a hostile reception, particularly in Scotland', wrote the Minister in his diary. 'HM remarked that all his predecessors had succeeded to the throne after their predecessors had died. "Mine is not only alive, but very much so." He thought it better for the Duke to proceed to Paris at once.'

The Windsors did however spend two further weeks in England, during which the Duke received his instructions and attended to such matters as uniforms (his new post involving demotion from his previous rank of Field Marshal to that of Major-General). During this time the British press were instructed by the censorship authorities not to mention them. Nevertheless, the Duke received many thousands of letters, 94 per cent of which were favourable.

They made a sad pilgrimage to the Fort. Before abdicating, the Duke had been promised that he might one day return to live there; but this now seemed unlikely, and the house and garden were in a sorry state. Sibyl Colefax, one of the few hostesses who had not 'ratted' on them after the Abdication, gave a lunch for them in London. In spite of the unhappy treatment they had received, they seemed in good spirits. Harold Nicolson noted in his diary: 'I have seldom seen the Duke in such cheerful spirits and it was rather touching to witness their delight at being back in England. There was no false note.' Geoffrey Madan found the Duke 'happily married to a devoted wife, not his equal but doing her best to live up to him'.

Above The Duke with Lord
Louis Mountbatten aboard the
HMS *Kelly*, September 1939.

Right Smiling for the press on
their first day back in England,
13 September 1939.

Above The Duchess and her friend Lady Mendl knitting for the French troops.

Below The Duchess receiving the gratitude of French officers for her charitable efforts. She wrote that none of the English war charities had invited her help – 'so time and money have gone to the French'.

In Paris the Duke reported to his Mission, which was based at the French GHQ at the Château de Vincennes. Meanwhile the Duchess reopened the house in the Boulevard Suchet, though they used only one floor and sent much of the furniture that they had spent the past year collecting into store. Her original thought had been to return to the South of France in order to turn La Cröe into a military hospital; but the Duke could not bear to be parted from her, and so she looked for a chance to do her bit in the capital. On 13 October she wrote to Aunt Bessie that she was 'involved in all sorts of war work – from giving artists lunch for 1 franc . . . to wrapping up parcels for soldiers at the front. . . .' Her friend Lady Mendl had started a charity sending clothes to the French troops, and the Duchess became much involved in this, as well as in the motorized section of the French Red Cross, delivering medical supplies to the front and getting within the sound of gunfire. She wrote to Sibyl Colefax that none of the English war charities in Paris had asked her to help – 'so time and money have gone to the French'.

With her indefatigable energy and innate organizing ability, the Duchess was an effective war worker; but she was angry at what she regarded as the indignities heaped upon her husband and the failure to make proper use of his talents. In November 1939, for example, while visiting British troops, he was reprimanded after taking a salute meant for his brother, the Duke of Gloucester. Describing this incident in her memoirs, the Duchess wrote that 'we had two wars to deal with – the big and still leisurely war, in which everybody was caught up, and the little war from the Palace, in which no quarter was given'. The Duke had always had a gift for inspiring troops. 'It seemed to me tragic that this unique gift . . . was never called upon, out of fear . . . that it might once more shine brightly, too brightly.' When the King visited the front soon afterwards, the Duchess wrote to her aunt: 'My brother-in-law arrives tomorrow, but competition still exists in the English mind – so one must hide so there is no rivalry. All very childish except that the biggest men take it seriously. Anyway the Duke can leave the front and spend those days with me so that the cheers are guaranteed.'

Social life continued intermittently and the Duchess did wonders in spite of limited supplies and electricity. On Christmas Eve they had a party for thirty at the Boulevard Suchet. The Duke came downstairs in his kilt playing the bagpipes, and Noël Coward sang *Mad Dogs and Englishmen*.

Above Celebrating Christmas with the Free Poles, December 1939.

Below On leave at La Cröe, March 1940.

On 30 December the Duchess wrote to Sibyl Colefax: 'Everything goes on the same here except that though the Duke wears the uniform the same Palace vendetta goes on making the job difficult and nearly impossible. . . . We are both thoroughly disgusted and fed up in every way but caught like rats in a trap until the war ends.' To her aunt she wrote in the New Year: 'The Duke's job is ridiculous and instead of using him where he might help the cause due to jealousy which even the death of men can't temper he has a childish job.' In fact, the Duchess was wrong. Though she did not know it, the Duke's job was important, since he was one of the few Englishmen to have a free run of the French defences; and he wrote some perceptive reports on their inadequacies, unfortunately ignored by British military intelligence. His situation was odd however in that, despite his unique access to the French Army, he was virtually prohibited from visiting the British Army in France.

On 10 May the Germans invaded. On the 15th, the Duchess wrote to her aunt: 'Paris so far seems all right and I want to stay with the Duke as long as possible and his job is here. . . . We have never had such a beautiful spring – one cannot believe there is so much misery and death about.' The Duke in fact found himself with little to do; but he was in a position to know about the disaster overtaking the allied armies. As always, his main concern was for his wife. On the 16th, he obtained leave to evacuate her to Biarritz. A week later, his commanding officer being positively anxious to get rid of him, he obtained a transfer to the Italian frontier: driving through refugee-choked roads, he collected the Duchess at Biarritz and took her to Antibes, where they re-installed themselves at La Cröe.

On 10 June Italy declared war on the Allies. The Duchess wrote to her aunt from La Cröe: 'It really is becoming a most awful mess. We haven't decided what we will do exactly. . . . I had just taken two Italian servants. . . . The Duke is with the army here for the moment . . . thinks the defences in the Alps excellent. . . .' On 19 June, however, with the French suing for an armistice, and the risk that the ex-King might be interned as a British officer or even captured by the enemy, the British Consul in Nice advised the Windsors to join his convoy which was about to leave for neutral Spain. They left amid many tears, the Duke presenting a final bouquet of flowers from the villa's garden to the Duchess, who had forgotten that it was her forty-fourth birthday.

The journey was long and complicated, and it was only with difficulty that

This exquisite flamingo brooch by Cartier, set in rubies, sapphires, emeralds and diamonds, was given by the Duke to the Duchess at Easter 1940.

the Duke persuaded the Spanish authorities to let him cross the frontier. Finally, they arrived in Barcelona, from where the Duke telegraphed his old friend Churchill, now Prime Minister: 'Having received no instructions have arrived in Spain to avoid capture. Proceeding to Madrid.' On 23 June they arrived in the Spanish capital, where they stayed at the Ritz and were looked after by British Ambassador Sir Samuel Hoare, an old friend.

Churchill wanted them to return to Britain, but the Duke, remembering the insulting treatment they had received in September, declared that he would do so only if he and his wife were received by the King and Queen. Otherwise he would be willing to serve anywhere in the Empire. Hoare urged the Duke to return without conditions; but he also urged the King to agree to the Duke's request, which amounted to very little, just a 'once only' meeting 'of a quarter of an hour'. Meanwhile the Windsors moved on to Portugal on 2 July. Hoare was glad to see them go, though he wrote to the Foreign Secretary Lord Halifax that they had 'made themselves extremely popular with the many Spaniards whom they have met'. Their visit had 'stimulated German propaganda but otherwise it has done good in extending our personal contacts'.

In Portugal the Windsors stayed at the villa of a Portuguese banker in Cascais near Lisbon, found for them by the British Embassy. An impatient message from Churchill was awaiting the Duke, threatening him with court martial if he did not return to England. Much upset, the Duke agreed to do so; but his telegram crossed with another from the Prime Minister, this time offering him the governorship of the Bahamas. According to the Duchess's memoirs the Duke declared that it was 'one of the few parts of the Empire I missed on my travels. It's a small governorship and three thousand miles from the war. Well, Winston said he was sorry, but it was the best he could do, and I shall keep my side of the bargain.'

Naturally, the Duchess did not consider her husband's new post flattering. She wrote to Aunt Bessie on 15 July:

We have nothing but a few suitcases packed in a hurry – a fine looking pair to arrive in Nassau. The St Helena of 1940 I hear is a nice spot. At least the British have got the Duke as far as possible. We refused to return to England except on our own terms, as the Duke is quite useless to the country if he was to receive the same treatment as when he returned to

Inspecting civil war ruins near Madrid, June 1940.

offer his services wholeheartedly in Sept only to suffer one humiliation after another. . . . So he asked for something out of England and he got it! . . . Can you fancy a family continuing a feud when the very Empire is threatened and not putting every man in a spot where he would be most useful? Could anything be so small and hideous? What will happen to a country which allows such behaviour?

The Duchess entertaining Portuguese ladies in the garden of the villa at Cascais where the Windsors spent the month of July 1940 awaiting the ship that was to take them to the Bahamas. In the top left-hand corner, obscured, is Walter Monckton, sent out by Churchill to warn them of Nazi plots and ensure they left on schedule.

There can be no doubt that, by this time, the Windsors felt bitter at their treatment, and also that the Duke was indiscreet in suggesting to friends that Britain seemed to have little chance of resisting a German invasion and would do well to contemplate peace negotiations. This was indeed what many Englishmen felt, including members of the cabinet, but it was unwise to voice such feelings at a time when the country was preparing to fight for its life. The Duchess was also unwise in arranging, through a Spanish diplomat friend, to

Passenger list of the SS *Excalibur* on which the Windsors sailed for the Bahamas on 1 August 1940.

have diplomatic protection conferred on their house in German-occupied Paris, and her maid sent there to pick up quantities of linen and other things they would be needing in the Bahamas. (The maid was eventually detained by the Germans who hoped the Duchess would refuse to sail without her.) One must however remember that the Windsors were very isolated and friendless at this time, that they had been through some rather odd experiences and were understandably feeling confused.

That July, while the Windsors were waiting to leave for the Bahamas, Ribbentrop, who had been encouraged by reports of the Duke's defeatist remarks, hatched a plot to stop him and the Duchess leaving Europe and to lure them into German hands by trickery. A Spanish friend of the Windsors, Miguel Primo de Rivera, went out to see them in Cascais. Primo de Rivera later reported to the German Ambassador in Madrid that the Windsors 'do not fear the King, who is utterly stupid, so much as the clever Queen, who is said to intrigue constantly against the Duke and particularly against the Duchess'. But when he suggested to the ex-King that he ought to remain in Europe as 'he might yet be destined to play a large part in English politics and even to ascend the English throne, both the Duke and Duchess seemed astonished. Both seemed completely enmeshed in conventional ways of thinking, for they replied that under the English constitution this would not be possible after the Abdication.' When Primo de Rivera said that the war might produce changes in the English constitution, 'the Duchess in particular became very thoughtful'.

Through Spanish and Portuguese agents the Germans tried various ploys to prevent the Windsors leaving for the Bahamas, but in spite of all the Duke and Duchess sailed on 1 August aboard the American steamer *Excalibur*, the boat by which they had always meant to travel. A few days earlier they had been joined by Walter Monckton, who had been sent out by Churchill to warn them of German designs on them and stress the need for prompt departure. 'I am so furious I can't see you as we are not coming to NY but that bloody Government won't let us come to the US', wrote the Duchess to her aunt during the sea journey. (The boat had been re-routed via Bermuda to prevent them passing through America at a politically sensitive time.) 'Naturally we loathe the job but it was the only way out of a difficult situation. . . . I miss my houses so terribly and can only think of returning to the irritating French – I could kiss them all now. . . .'

At Fort Charlotte, Nassau, 23 August 1940.

CHAPTER NINE

'Feeling so far away'

1940–45   The Bahamas in 1940 did not have the glamorous image they would subsequently acquire. They constituted one of the most backward colonies of the British Empire, with a population of only 70,000 and virtually no agriculture. A decade earlier, the fragile economy had been based on bootlegging during American Prohibition, and only in the mid-1930s did the capital, Nassau on New Providence Island, start to acquire a reputation as a smart winter resort for American visitors. Economic and political power was in the hands of the Bay Street Boys, a mafia of tough white merchants, descended from the original pirate settlers, who controlled the local legislature and consistently opposed the colonial government as it sought to reform the economy and improve the lot of the black majority.

The Windsors were given a tremendous welcome by the local population, but otherwise the circumstances of their arrival in mid-August 1940 were not calculated to inspire them with confidence. They were almost suffocated by the extreme heat and humidity; they discovered Government House in a near-derelict state; and they found themselves exposed to the full glare of the American press. Their position in provincial local society was complicated by their difference in status, emphasized by an official telegram which had preceded them instructing that no lady was to curtsy to the Duchess. They also experienced a violent culture shock after coming from war-torn Europe: the war had hardly yet impinged on the Bahamas, next to the still-neutral United States.

The Duchess's letters to her aunt that summer and autumn reveal their private disenchantment with their new post. 'I can't get used to being so far from the war', she wrote on 31 August. 'I really would have preferred air raids in England to feeling so far away.' On 16 September she wrote: 'The heat is *awful*. I long for some air that isn't caused by electric fans. . . . I hate this place more each day.' On 25 October she wrote: 'One might as well be in London with all the bombs and excitement and not buried alive here.' And on 21 November: 'We both hate it and the locals are petty-minded, the visitors common and uninteresting.' Meanwhile the Duke, to let off steam, drafted (but did not send) an indignant letter to Winston Churchill about the difficulties of his post, which he saw as a banishment brought about by 'the vindictive jealousy of a few royal women. . . .'.

However, the Windsors did not show their feelings and uncomplainingly got down to their official duties. The Duke was determined to solve the local unemployment problem and reduce the over-reliance of the economy on tourism. After he had opened the annual session of the House of Assembly at the end of October, the United States Consul noted that his speech had been

one of the most sensible and business-like that has been delivered by a Governor for many years. It . . . indicates that the Duke is already familiar

Arrival at Nassau on 17 August 1940, aboard the *Lady Somers* from Bermuda.

with local conditions and has a determination to improve those conditions. . . . It may be true that he and his Duchess were sent here to get rid of them, so to speak, but he is taking his job seriously and is showing a keen interest in the welfare of the Bahamas.

Meanwhile the Duchess involved herself with her usual energy in the local Red Cross and other charities, and also devoted herself to the refurbishment of Government House. As she told the American journalist Adela St Johns:

Don't you see, I must make a home for him? That's why I'm doing this place over, so we can live in it with comfort as a home. All his life he has travelled, and a place to come back to is not always a home. The only one he ever had he made for himself at Fort Belvedere. He had to leave it – you don't know what that meant to him. I must make him a home. . . .

Welcoming ceremony at Fort Charlotte, 23 August 1940, one of the few official occasions on which the Windsors were photographed with the coloured people of the colony, towards whom the Duke took a paternalistic attitude.

To her aunt she wrote on 16 September that 'Isabel Price [a New York decorator] came down here and together we are going to dish this shack up so that at least one isn't ashamed of asking the local horrors here'. The house was rebuilt with the aid of £5,000 reluctantly voted by the House of Assembly, while the Windsors paid for the interior redecoration themselves.

For the Windsors the Bahamas did have one important advantage – its close proximity to the United States, which they both looked forward to visiting. The Duchess had not seen her native country since 1933, while the Duke had not been there since 1927. Traditionally, the Governor of the Bahamas spent his summers on the mainland and exchanged visits with the Mayor of Miami, a city only 180 miles from Nassau. The British Government was not however keen for the Duke to leave his post, fearing that he might make some indiscreet remark about the war which would affect Anglo-American relations at a critical moment. The thought that he might have a successful reception there was equally distasteful to the Royal Family and their Court who did not wish him to have any kind of personal success. He was ordered to keep out of the United States at least until the Presidential Elections in November; but even after these, he received no permission to leave the Bahamas. 'I think we are fated never to go to America', wrote the Duchess to her aunt. 'Great Britain hates the idea of our going, because you know the Duke is an independent thinker and they don't want him to open his mouth. . . .'

At the end of November the Duchess had some dental trouble and was advised by the Nassau dentists to seek treatment in Miami. Much to the Duke's surprise, he was told that they might go there for this purpose for five specified days in mid-December. Unknown to them, the newly re-elected President Roosevelt was due to visit Bahamian waters during these days aboard a US warship, to inspect a proposed American base site on the island of Mayaguana: although he expressed a wish to meet the Duke, the British Government was anxious that no such meeting should take place, so it suited it to have the Windsors leave the colony. In fact the ploy failed, as the President sent his private plane to Miami to fly the Duke out to his ship: Roosevelt, though aware of the Duke's ambiguous views on the war, was fascinated by the man who had given up his throne for love, and the two men were to meet quite often during the next four years and to become friends.

Meanwhile, the journey to Miami showed that the Windsors were in fact

The Duchess with the ladies of the Bahamas Red Cross.

extremely popular in America and a good wartime advertisement for Britain there. Twelve thousand people turned out to greet them on their arrival, headed by a reception committee of the State Governor and four mayors. While the Duchess was in hospital, the Duke (as the British Consul recalled) 'never missed an opportunity to perform some act of public relations in aid of the British war effort. . . . A holiday atmosphere prevailed; Britain's stock soared with the advent to Miami of our former monarch. I remember recording in my despatch to the Foreign Office that the visit had been "a success from every point of view". This was no exaggeration.'

When the Windsors returned from Miami, the elegantly refurbished Government House was ready for their occupation, and the winter tourist season was about to begin. Thanks to the glamorous presence of the Royal Governor and his American Duchess, this was to be the best the Bahamas had

On their first visit to Miami in December 1940, with the Mayor, Mr Orr.

yet known: 20,000 people came over from the mainland, compared with 14,000 the year before, and the amount of dollars spent in the colony increased by a similar proportion. The Windsors did not relish presiding over a tourist paradise – 'it goes against the grain', the Duke had written to Churchill, 'to play the part of "greeter" amidst all the horrors and misery that this war inflicts' – but did what was expected of them. Although they entertained prominent visitors in the dignified surroundings of their new residence, they refused all social invitations except to those events that were in aid of war charities, and the funds raised on these occasions were impressive.

At the end of March 1941 the Windsors made a boat tour of the Out Islands – islands other than New Providence: it was the first time a Governor had ever visited these places, all of which were primitive and impoverished. To alleviate their worst hardships, the Duke set up a 'Bahamas Assistance Fund', to which he made over the income from a trust he had founded as Prince of Wales. This was run by the Duchess, who also ran two infant welfare clinics in Nassau to reduce the high infant mortality rate among the black population. Although she never lost the characteristic prejudices of her Southern birth, sometimes writing to her aunt of 'lazy, thriving niggers', she spent much time at these clinics caring for the babies and saving lives.

The Windsors had hoped to visit the mainland during the summer of 1941, but this was vetoed by Churchill, who had been annoyed by an interview the Duke had given to an American magazine in which he had expressed sentiments which might have been construed as mildly defeatist. In the autumn, however, after the Duke had written to the Prime Minister assuring him of his loyalty and discretion, they were finally allowed to leave for six weeks. Apart from ten days of genuine holiday on the Duke's Canadian ranch, they visited Washington, where they were entertained by the President, Maryland, where the Duchess saw her family for the first time in eight years, and New York. Everywhere they were greeted by wild and enthusiastic crowds: in Washington these were larger than the crowds that had welcomed the King and Queen on their state visit in June 1939. In New York they were treated to a ticker tape storm; and in Baltimore the Duchess was mobbed as a returning daughter of that city.

Since the Duke's uncle Lord Athlone, the Governor-General of Canada, refused to receive the Duchess, their journey to Alberta did not follow the

Above Government House, Nassau, after its refurbishment.

Opposite above The Duchess's drawing room showing her famous pre-war portrait by Gerald Brockhurst.

Opposite below The Duke's bed-sitting room.

Above Two snapshots of the Duchess in Nassau.

Below The Duchess tries out deep-sea fishing during the Windsors' first tour of the Out Islands in March 1941.

usual route through Ottawa but crossed the American Mid-West, which was notoriously anti-British. Here if anywhere the Windsors might have expected to receive a hostile reception; but even in Chicago, the home of Isolationism, their reception was rapturous. In the still-neutral United States, the Windsors went out of their way to do their bit for the British war effort. The Duke presented wings to Canadian pilots, the Duchess visited wounded British merchant seamen in Baltimore. In New York they made widely-publicized visits to many of the organizations involved in British war relief.

After their return to Nassau in November, the Duchess wrote to Aunt Bessie:

> We both simply took to our beds on arrival and recovered quietly from the strenuous trip, which the papers called a *vacation*! We had 2 days in Miami where I was able to go into a shop with a *fair* amount of peace. . . . Nassau is like a deflated soufflé after this trip and it is hard to settle down to our jobs and to the neutrality of a village. . . . I am sure I am better off on excitement – it's boredom that gets me down. Mother always used to say that about me. . . .

However, within a month life ceased to be boring, thanks to the entry of the United States into the war following Pearl Harbor. 'I am glad we are going to be *in* the war', wrote the Duchess to her aunt, 'which is better than being on the outside. This place is going to be isolated . . . and everything will be very curtailed.' With the collapse of the tourist trade the Bahamas faced an economic crisis, resulting in new responsibilities both for the Duke as Governor and the Duchess in her charitable work.

In 1940 the Windsors had been depressed by the fact that the Bahamas were an unimportant backwater and far removed from the war. In 1942 the colony ceased to be either of these things, and life became very eventful for the Royal Governor and his wife. It was decided, thanks partly to the Duke's persuasive efforts, to set up two important RAF bases on New Providence, to be constructed by American firms employing local labour. This solved the local unemployment problem and promised Nassau a busy future as a war station. In June 1942, while the Duke was absent in Washington discussing the colony's needs with the United States Government, labour riots broke out, the result of

Right & below The Duchess
disembarks after her first aeroplane
journey, when the Windsors made
a flying visit to Palm Beach in
April 1941.

Opposite above On the E. P. Ranch
in Alberta, Canada, September
1941, with the Stony Indians.

Opposite below The Duchess meets
Eleanor Roosevelt at the Civilian
Defense Headquarters in
Washington, 28 October 1941

Above At a forces club in New York, 1943.

Right With Major Hayes of the US Corps of Engineers, at the construction site near Nassau of the RAF base subsequently known as Windsor Field.

low standard wages which the House of Assembly had refused to raise in spite of the Duke's requests. Flying back to Nassau, he quickly calmed the situation; and during the months that followed, he finally achieved a political ascendancy over the Bay Street Boys who had been trying to frustrate his reforming efforts.

By the spring of 1943 the new bases were completed and smoothly running. Nassau was filled with servicemen, fed at a canteen which the Duchess personally managed. Many important people passed through and were superbly entertained at Government House, where they were impressed by the Duke's grasp of events. The impoverished inhabitants of the Out Islands were able, under a scheme devised by the Duke in discussions with American officials, to work on farms that were short of labour on the American mainland, remitting unheard-of wages to their families at home. The Duke and Duchess were popular with everyone and generally thought to have done well under difficult circumstances: they hoped their success would be rewarded with the offer of another, more important job for the Duke.

In May 1943 the Windsors made another visit to the United States, where they met Churchill, who was in Washington as the guest of the President. They were present when Churchill addressed Congress – on which occasion the Duke received more applause than the Prime Minister, who seemed annoyed by the fact. In private talks with Churchill, the Duke asked for the promotion he felt he deserved. He was probably hoping that the British Government would recommend him for the vacant Governor-Generalship of Australia, but when he next heard from Churchill on 10 June it was only to be offered the Governorship of Bermuda. This the Duke rejected, writing to his solicitor George Allen that 'Winston does not seem to have got my meaning of a move'. Though fractionally higher in the colonial pecking order, Bermuda was even smaller than the Bahamas, and five hundred miles from the American mainland, whereas Nassau's proximity to the United States was 'one of the distinct benefits of life on this otherwise lousy little island on which we have been marooned for far too long'.

'I am convinced the Duke was perfectly correct to refuse', wrote the Duchess to her aunt. 'I can't see much point in island jumping. I'm for the big hop to a mainland.' In her memoirs she afterwards wrote: 'It was now clear beyond question that David's family were determined to keep him relegated to the furthermost marches of the Empire.' To the Duchess it was always evident that

The Duke posing on a Nassau beach with muscle-flexing American soldiery.

they had the Court, and particularly her sister-in-law, to thank for their difficulties and frustrations. In an exasperated letter to Aunt Bessie of March 1941,
she had cursed their banishment, attributing it to 'a woman's jealousy and a
country's fear his brother wouldn't shine if he [the Duke] was there!' But in
one sense the Duchess was mistaken. The Queen had not been responsible for
sending them to the Bahamas and had in fact been against the post, thinking it
too good for them. In July 1940 she had written to Lord Lloyd, Secretary of
State for the Colonies, that the Duchess was unfit even to be a governor's wife.

The Duke's relations with his family were now so bad that almost no com-
munication passed between them for two years. As he later wrote to the King,
'ever since I returned to England in 1939 to offer my services and you continued to persecute [me] and then frustrate my modest efforts to serve you and my
country in war, I must frankly admit that I have become very bitter indeed'.
Only when his favourite brother, George, Duke of Kent, was killed in an aeroplane accident in August 1942 was there some resumption of correspondence
in the family's united grief. 'It is a most tragic death, and I think his services
will be greatly missed by Great Britain', wrote the Duchess to her aunt. (As
noted in Chapter Three, she had seen quite a lot of the Kents around the time
of their marriage in 1934.) 'He was the one with the most charm left at the job
– and they made a couple more up with the advances of this world – in spite of
the "turn coat" to us. We are both greatly shocked and distressed and it is so
sad for her and the 3 little children.' But the warm family letters exchanged at
this time of mourning did not lead to any change in the attitude of the Royal
Family towards the Windsors; indeed, the Duke was reminded that, as a result
of the family feud, he had not even been allowed to meet Prince George when
the latter visited the United States a year earlier. And when the Duke, submit-
ting the annual Bahamas honours list at the end of 1942, asked if the King
might at last admit royal rank to the Duchess 'in recognition of her two years'
public service in the Bahamas', the reply was an uncompromising negative.

Ironically, the Royal Family were able to get personal news of the Duke
thanks to the Duchess, who had the boldness to write to Queen Mary, using as
her courier John Dauglish, the retiring Bishop of Nassau. 'It has always been a
source of sorrow and regret to me that I have been the cause of any separation
which exists between Mother and Son', she wrote, with a touch of irony, 'and I
can't help but feel that there must be moments, however fleeting they may be,

when you wonder how David is.' The Bishop, who was returning to England, having been an invaluable support to the Windsors on their 'tiny isle', would be able to tell the Queen 'if all the things David gave up are replaced to him in another way and the little details of his daily life. . . . The horrors of war and the endless separation of families have in my mind stressed the importance of family ties.' Eventually, the Queen summoned the Bishop to Badminton in Gloucestershire, where she was spending the war with her retinue of fifty-five, and listened with attention to all he had to say about the Duke in the Bahamas; but when he began to talk praisingly about the Duchess and her good work, he met 'a stone wall of disinterest'. Queen Mary did however astonish the Duke (who knew nothing of his wife's letter) by sending 'a kind message' to the Duchess when she next wrote to her son.

On 8 July 1943, soon after the Duke had turned down the Bermuda offer, Sir Harry Oakes, the Canadian gold millionaire who was the Bahamas' richest resident, was murdered in his sleep at Westbourne, his mansion outside Nassau. Oakes was a friend of the Windsors, who had been his guests at Westbourne while Government House was being rebuilt in the autumn of 1940, and had since relied on his help in many of their charitable and other schemes. The murder (apparently by 'torching') was beyond the capacity of the local police, who were already discredited after their failure to deal with the riots of the previous year, and the Duke took the unfortunate step of calling in two leading detectives of the Miami police force who had efficiently organized his personal security during his visits to that city. In his eagerness to deliver the goods, one of the detectives proceeded to 'cook' the evidence against the principal suspect, Oakes' unpopular and dissolute son-in-law, Alfred de Marigny, and the inept manner in which he did so ensured de Marigny's acquittal when the case was heard the following October. The unsolved murder intensified the air of gangsterism that had always been present in the colony, whose original settlers had been pirates. 'We are endeavouring to keep as clear from this awful case as is possible', wrote the Duchess to her aunt. 'I am afraid there is a lot of dirt underneath and I think the natives are all protecting themselves from the exposure of business deals – strange drums of petrol etc. – so I wonder how far it will all go. Most unpleasant as I do not think there is a big enough laundry anywhere to take Nassau's dirty linen.'

Despite such frightful episodes, the many annoying elements of life in the

Bahamas, and the constant sense of being employed in a role beneath their talents, their five years there were a happy time for the Windsors during which they could pride themselves on many positive achievements. The Duke became very much the master of his little fiefdom and to some extent was able to mould it according to his ideas: he managed to win over hostile local politicians by a mixture of cunning tactics and flattering use of hospitality and the honours system. It must be admitted that, while he sought to improve the lot of the black population, he did little to change the local 'colour bar'; but this was more entrenched in the Bahamas than in any other colony, and he would not have been able to do much about it even had he been minded to (which he was probably not, being an old-fashioned paternalist who regarded the 'coloured' people as 'children'). In his domestic life he was very happy. The Duchess supported him by running his house in a manner befitting an ex-King, and doing everything that might be expected of a Governor's wife and more. She saw to it that he was always punctual and attended to his duties in an efficient and dignified manner. He was very proud of her, and always insisted that she be treated as his equal in the Bahamas, where few begrudged her the honours due to royalty.

During the later stages of the war, the Duke naturally began to think of what he would do and where they would live in future. Being only fifty years of age in 1944, he hoped to be offered another official job in peacetime, and wanted particularly to act as some kind of cultural ambassador for Britain in America, for he greatly enjoyed being in the United States and got on extremely well with most Americans: he believed he had already made a number of important converts among former isolationists and could contribute further to Anglo-American relations. (An additional motive in seeking such a job was that the Windsors would not have been able to afford to live in America in the style to which they were accustomed without the tax privileges that would have resulted from diplomatic status.) Churchill was sympathetic to the Duke's desire, but unable to arrange anything of this or any other nature owing to opposition both from the Palace (which did not want the Duke to have any further kudos) and the civil service (whose natural reluctance to contemplate the creation of unusual public positions was heightened in the case of an ex-King who was on obvious bad terms with his family and whose wife had an embarrassingly peculiar status). The Duke also hoped that his family would receive the Duchess if only once, which if not restoring normal family relations would at least put an end to the endless comment to the effect that the Windsors were outcasts. As he wrote to Churchill in October 1944:

> Were the King and Queen to behave normally to the Duchess and myself when we pass by England, and invite us merely to tea at one of their residences, a formality which as a matter of fact is prescribed by Court protocol in the case of Colonial Governors and their wives, it would prevent any division of feeling being manifested. . . . It could never be a very happy meeting, but it would be quite painless, and would have the merit of silencing once and for all those who delight in keeping open an eight-year-old wound that ought to have been healed officially, if not privately, years ago.

Churchill replied that he had tried his best, but that the King and Queen, particularly the latter, refused, to the Prime Minister's regret, to receive the Duchess under any circumstances.

On holiday in Virginia, 1944.

At the rue de la Faisanderie, 1949.

CHAPTER TEN

'Homeless on the face of the earth'

1945–53   *I*n May 1947 Harold Nicolson met
the Windsors on one of their rare
visits to London. He found the Duke
looking much happier and healthier than before the war, and the Duchess
much softer – 'that taut predatory look has gone'. She took him aside and
explained that their great problem was deciding where to live. 'We are tired of
wandering. We are not as young as we were. We want to settle down and grow
our own trees. He likes gardening, but it is no fun gardening in other people's
gardens. . . .' Nicolson felt 'really sorry for them. She was so simple and
sincere.'

The problem of where to settle troubled the Windsors for almost six years
after their departure from the Bahamas in May 1945. The choice seemed to lie
between France, England and the United States. Each country had its attrac-
tions but also its serious drawbacks. As before the war, they were welcome
guests in France, where they enjoyed tax and other privileges, and the Duchess
adored the gracious living; the Duke, while less happy there, found it conve-
niently close to England and his English friends; but the country was in a state
of disorder and uncertainty after the war and occupation and promised to
remain so for some time. They returned there in 1945, to rejoin their houses
and possessions and because they had nowhere else to go; but they did not
expect to remain there for long. As for England, the Duke yearned to return
there, to live for at least part of each year at his beloved Fort Belvedere; there
was no good political reason why he should not do so, ten years after the
Abdication; but life there promised to be uncomfortable unless he managed to
achieve a measure of reconciliation with his family and recognition for his wife.
Failing England, America was the Duke's preferred choice; he felt greatly at
home there and enjoyed the openness and affluence of American society; and
although the Duchess was not keen on settling in the United States, particularly

on account of the press, she would have been prepared to do so for her husband's sake. But life there would be too expensive unless the Duke secured the British diplomatic post he wanted, which would have brought him a tax-free status and a contribution to his expenses.

Having spent the summer in America, the Windsors sailed for France on 15 September 1945 in an atmosphere of uncertainty. They were relieved to find their house on the Boulevard Suchet much as they had left it, though dismayed to learn that it had been sold during the summer and they would have to move out by April 1946. Meanwhile, despite food and electricity shortages, the Duchess set about making it a place of lively entertainment, adding a touch of brightness to the rather dismal Paris scene that winter. Their guests included pre-war French acquaintances, their friends the Duff Coopers who were now at the British Embassy, and British and American officers stationed in Paris. On 25 January the Duchess wrote to her aunt that they had given a successful party to 'cheer up' several dozen friends at a nervous moment after General de Gaulle's resignation, the hospitality consisting of 'a buffet of hot dogs from the US, ham mousse from tinned ham, salade russe from tinned vegetables, sandwiches of cheese & cresson and black market eggs stuffed', along with three bottles of whisky and thirty of champagne. But despite such jolly episodes, the Duchess was worried about her husband, who was bored and fretful and had pitifully little to do.

In October 1945 the Duke had visited London alone to see if he could secure both family reconciliation and official work of some kind, preferably the post after which he hankered as a goodwill ambassador to the United States. The Duchess was anxious for him to find employment, and concerned that he should not prejudice his chances by insisting on her 'recognition'. He stayed with his mother, whom he had not seen since 1936; their reunion was amicable, as were the Duke's meetings with other members of his family and of the new Labour Government. The King was not averse to giving him the job he wanted in America, fearing that otherwise he might return to live in England, a course to which George VI made it clear he was resolutely opposed. There was also talk of making him ambassador to a distant power such as Argentina, or governor of a middle-ranking colony such as Ceylon. But as Ziegler shows, every proposal was sabotaged by the King's Private Secretary Sir Alan Lascelles, who represented the old Court establishment which had not forgiven the Duke for

Bitter-sweet reunion of mother and son, October 1945.

having abdicated. Nor was there any lessening in the royal hostility towards the Duchess, though the Duke prudently did not mention her when discussing his desire for work.

By the time the Windsors left the Boulevard Suchet in the spring of 1946, it seemed unlikely that the Duke would be offered any official post. 'I would not feel so down about the future if we could remain here in this lovely house', wrote the Duchess, 'but it is finding a place and beginning again which is so dreary. . . .' For the time being, they decided to move to La Cröe, which had also miraculously escaped serious damage, and which the Duchess quickly restored to its pre-war magnificence: with its staff of twenty-seven, she imagined that 'outside of embassies it is the only house run in this fashion in France and probably England today'. They were able to live in such style thanks to the Duchess's housekeeping talents and the Duke's ability to obtain food and drink from local British military authorities. While the Duchess missed the bustle of Paris, the Duke seemed happier on the Riviera, where he enjoyed his golf and other outdoor pursuits; they also had interesting neighbours, including other exiled royals, and many of their English friends came out there to escape the post-war gloom.

Between the autumn of 1946 and the spring of 1948 the Windsors, while keeping La Cröe as their base, experimented with life both in England and the United States. They made two extended visits to England; and while they enjoyed seeing old friends, they did not feel encouraged to return to live there. The first visit was marred by the theft of the Duchess's jewellery while they were staying with the Duke's old friend Lord Dudley. They found life uncomfortably changed from before the war, owing to the regime of austerity and financial stringency instituted by the Labour Government. The one thing that continued to tempt the Duke back was Fort Belvedere; at the time of the Abdication, George VI had promised to keep this for the Duke's eventual return. In February 1947 the Duchess (it is significant that the letter came from her and not the Duke) wrote from Palm Beach to their solicitor George Allen that they were thinking of buying a house there for the winter 'if *only* we could have the Fort for the autumn and spring. . . . We would not be there long enough to upset the powers that be, and we in our old age could have 2 nice houses where we want them. . . . It is a waste of time being homeless on the face of the earth and most disturbing. . . .' However, the King, who dreaded the

Above The Windsors on one of their rare visits to England, May 1947, with their hostess Mrs Parkinson. They were staying only a mile from the Fort, to which they still hoped to return.

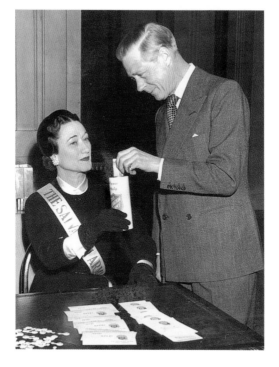

Right The Duke contributes $100 to the Duchess's collection box at a fund-raising event at the Waldorf Astoria, February 1950.

Duke's return to England in any form, refused to allow him the Fort, which was eventually let on a commercial lease to the Duke's nephew Gerald Lascelles (a distant cousin of the King's Private Secretary). The fact that the Windsors received no invitation to the wedding of Princess Elizabeth and Prince Philip in November 1947, the first important royal event since the Coronation, confirmed that they could expect to be cold-shouldered by the Royal Family in England for the foreseeable future.

The trips to America, where the Windsors went for a stay of several months in December 1946 and again the following year, basing themselves at the Waldorf Astoria in New York but also visiting Long Island, Palm Beach and their ranch in Canada, were far more successful: although persecuted by the press, notably the gossip columnists Elsa Maxwell and Walter Winchell, they were immensely popular there and lavishly entertained by many friends, who paid serious attention to the Duke's views and treated him with a mixture of respect and informality. The Duke was confirmed in his desire to go to live there, but they were uncomfortably aware that it would be impossible for them to keep up with the millionaires among whom they moved if they had to pay American taxes. Virtually all hope had now vanished of the diplomatic status which would have overcome this difficulty; and the Duke found it difficult as an ex-King to contemplate a job in the business world, though he seriously considered the offer of a directorship from his friend Robert Young, the railway tycoon. (As the Duchess said to Harold Nicolson, the Duke 'was born to be a salesman. . . . But an ex-King cannot start selling motor cars.')

When the Windsors returned to La Cröe from America in the summer of 1948, it was a time of international crisis, with the Berlin Blockade and the beginnings of the Cold War; so worried was the Duke at the prospect of a Soviet invasion of Western Europe that he had many of their possessions at La Cröe packed up and sent to store in America. He planned to follow them with the Duchess and take a two-year lease of a house on Long Island belonging to Eugène de Rothschild, his former host at Enzesfeld; but in the end he did not do so. He fell ill for a while; he felt their financial situation to be too precarious for the proposed move; and the Duchess was loth to leave her beloved France. In 1949 their wealthy French friend Paul-Louis Weiller offered to lend them his Paris town house in the rue de la Faisanderie for two years, an offer which the Windsors gratefully accepted, though the Duchess found the house gloomy and unimaginatively furnished, and its small dining room made entertainment difficult on a large scale. Nevertheless, displaying the talent that had transformed such unpromising properties as Bryanston Court and La Cröe, she managed to turn it into an elegant and comfortable showpiece. In September of that year the Windsors surrendered the lease of La Cröe with much regret.

By this time the Duke, much encouraged by his wife, had at last found an occupation to fill his days – the writing of his memoirs, which kept him busy from 1948 to 1951. He worked hard, covering thousands of pages with his clear handwriting, though he required an editor to help him put his material into publishable form: this was Charles Murphy, who had a difficult relationship with the Windsors, about whom he would later write a viciously disparaging book. To reminisce about the events of his former career, the Duke invited old friends to come out and stay with him at La Cröe and the rue de la Faisanderie, which gave him much pleasure. On the other hand, his study of the events of 1936 filled him with a renewed sense of grievance at the King's continuing refusal to allow his wife to share his royal status; and this led to a stand-up row with George VI in London in 1949, following which the two brothers had little more to do with each other.

The Duke's book was published in April 1951 under the title *A King's Story*: it was well received and became a bestseller on both sides of the Atlantic. It was around this time that the Windsors at last made a definite decision to base themselves in France for the rest of their lives. It no longer seemed likely, as the Duke had feared three years earlier, that the Russians would invade the West or the communists take control of the French Government. Nor was there any greater likelihood that the Duke would be offered a diplomatic position which would enable them to settle in America (though the return of Churchill to power at the end of 1951 slightly raised his hopes). And their return to live in England seemed more unlikely than ever in view of the latest flare-up of the old quarrel over the Duchess's title. Meanwhile, the substantial sums earned by the Duke from his memoirs meant they could think of establishing themselves in both a town and country house in France in appropriate style. They stayed on at the rue de la Faisanderie while they looked around for suitable properties. In the summer of 1952 they bought a beautiful though somewhat derelict old mill house in the valley of the Chevreuse, the Moulin de la Tuilerie, from their friend the artist Drian, and set about transforming it into

Dancing at Biarritz.

Opposite The Duchess did not
enjoy field sports but bravely
accompanied her husband on this
British regimental shoot in
Germany, November 1951.

Right Stylishly dressed in match-
ing checks, the Windsors prepare
to watch a golfing competition at
Saint-Cloud, 1953.

a comfortable rural retreat with an English garden, a task which would keep them busy for years. Then, in the spring of 1953, they acquired the lease from the City of Paris of 4 route du Champ d'Entraînement, a fine turn-of-the-century mansion in the Bois de Boulogne, and the stylish transformation of this house provided yet another happy occupation for their middle years.

The Windsors continued to winter each year in New York, where during the early fifties they saw much of Jimmy Donahue, the handsome Woolworth heir who was then in his mid-thirties. They had first met him with his mother in Nassau and Palm Beach in 1941, but only got to know him in the spring of 1950, when they liked him so well that they invited him to join them in France for several months. Donahue was witty and entertaining, as well as extremely generous, and both the Windsors came to enjoy his company immensely. At this period the Duke suffered from lumbago, was unable to dance, and tended to go to bed quite early; while the Duchess had reached a restless time of life and enjoyed late, boisterous parties at night clubs (a habit to which she had

With Jimmy Donahue in New York.

originally been introduced by the Duke in 1933). It was therefore Donahue who often escorted her to these establishments, a fact that did not unduly worry the Duke as the Duchess took care to be chaperoned and Donahue was well known to be homosexual. ('She's as safe as houses with *him*!') But the frequency with which they were seen together in public, often in high spirits, led to press speculation as to the stability of the Windsor marriage. No doubt the Duchess sometimes behaved foolishly with her flamboyant escort: he was a type who might sweep one off one's feet and cause one to lose one's head. Donahue for his part appears to have been genuinely fascinated by the Duchess, drawn perhaps by her masculinity; there was much talk that they might be having some kind of affair. By appealing to his wife, the Duke could have put an end to the friendship at any time: the fact that he did not do so for so long (the relationship cooled early in 1953 and ended in the summer of 1954) is an indication both of his personal liking for Donahue and his willingness to indulge the Duchess.

After more than a dozen years of marriage, the Duchess was undoubtedly feeling the strain of constant attention to the physical and emotional comfort of her royal husband, whose devotion could be exhausting, and of living down by discreet behaviour the disapproval she had aroused after the Abdication. She longed to enjoy again something of the adventure that had marked her early life, and her fling with Donahue, a colourful and daring personality who shared her quick wit, must be viewed in this light. Noël Coward, after meeting Donahue with the Windsors at a Mediterranean resort, concluded that it was his homosexuality which rendered him so attractive not only to the Duchess but also the Duke. There can be no doubt of the Duchess's preference for gay men: her favourite people included Cecil Beaton, Chips Channon, Somerset Maugham and indeed Coward himself; and many of her happiest moments were spent in the largely homosexual world of the great decorators and couturiers and upper servants. The Duke's personality and behaviour suggests that he possessed homosexual leanings, like his brother Prince George; his adoration of the Duchess would of itself indicate this; and while he certainly repressed any feelings he may have had where other men were concerned, some had the impression that he got at least a subliminal *frisson* out of Donahue's company.

In February 1952 the Windsors were wintering in New York when they learnt – characteristically from American journalists and not the British Embassy – of the death of King George VI. The Duke sailed for England to attend the funeral – a journey which, as he told the press, was all the sadder as he would have to undertake it alone, without his wife. It was a moment of acute depression for him, reminding him overwhelmingly of all the slights and difficulties he had experienced since the Abdication and of the long family estrangement. The Duchess did her best to keep up his spirits with loving letters, which naturally expressed the hope that the sad event, and the start of the new reign, would prove something of a turning point in their relations with the Royal Family in England.

'My own darling one', she wrote on 7 February, just after he had sailed, 'I hate not being with you at this time when you need me most and my place is by your side. I will be thinking of you every minute and holding your hand very tight and giving you all the courage I have to go through *gracefully* with this ordeal.' The following day she wrote: 'I hope everything won't be too hard and that for once a few decent things will come your way after the long, sad journey and the difficult relationships.' When the Duke arrived in England, he telephoned her to say that his family had given him quite a friendly reception. She wrote to him urging him to make the best of the conciliatory atmosphere:

> Now that the door has been opened a crack try and get your foot in, in the hope of making it even wider in future because that is best for WE. . . . I suggest that you see the widow and tell her . . . how difficult things have been for us and that also we have gone out of our way to keep our life dignified which has not been easy. . . . And leave it there. *Do not mention or ask for anything regarding recognition of me.* I am sure you can win her over to a more friendly attitude. . . . I know how you hate being there but this is a golden opportunity and it may only knock but once.

The Duchess was concerned that, in the funeral procession, the Duke should be given his proper place as the brother of the late sovereign: she was relieved to get a telegram from him reassuring her that this had been so. But hopes of a more general reconciliation were shattered when the Duke learned that the modest annuity paid to him by his brother, amounting to a little over £10,000, would not be continued during the new reign. 'I did feel so distressed hearing

The Duke walking in the funeral procession of King George VI, February 1952, flanked by
his brother the Duke of Gloucester and nephew the Duke of Kent

Above Crossing the Atlantic.

Below The Windsors with Princess Mary in New York, March 1953, the first time in fifteen years that the Duchess had met any member of her husband's family. The Duke and his sister were about to sail for England to attend their mother's deathbed.

your voice last night', she wrote to him on 17 February. 'They are beasts to continue to treat you the way they do. . . . I am afraid Mrs Temple Sr [a Windsor nickname for the Queen Mother] will never give in. . . .' He replied that her letters 'have been my only props on this difficult, painful and discouraging trip. . . . Cookie [the Queen Mother] was sugar . . . and M[ountbatten] and other relations and the Court officials correct and friendly on the surface. But gee the crust is hard & only granite below. . . . You'll never know how much I miss you, Peaches, and [I] just can't wait to get back to you and out of all this here. . . .'

A year later this drama was more or less repeated when, early in March 1953, the Duke learnt in New York that his mother was seriously ill. With a heavy heart, he sailed for England to see her for the last time. Once again the Duchess was effectively prohibited from accompanying him, but tried to keep up his spirits with letters which were maternal in tone. 'I worry so much about you because you are such a child when you are alone. . . . So much love my darling and keep your chin up and your tummy full.' In London the Duke made daily bedside visits to Queen Mary, who was sinking rapidly, though there was no telling how long she might last. 'It's one of the most trying situations I've ever found myself in', he wrote to the Duchess, 'and hanging around someone who has been so mean and vile to you my sweetheart is getting me down.'

The Duke could never forgive his mother for refusing to receive his wife despite his constant pleas. When she finally died, he wrote to the Duchess: 'My sadness was mixed with incredulity that any mother could have been so hard and cruel towards her eldest son for so many years and yet so demanding at the end without relenting a scrap. I'm afraid the fluids in her veins have always been as icy cold as they now are in death.' Nor were his feelings towards the rest of his family more generous. As he wrote to the Duchess after the funeral: 'What a smug, stinking lot my relations are and you've never seen what a seedy, worn-out bunch of old hags most of them have become. . . . I've been boiling mad the whole time that you haven't been here in your rightful place as a daughter-in-law at my side. But let us skip this rude interlude and enjoy our lovely full life together far removed from the boredom, the restrictions and the intrigues of the Royal Family and the Court. You just don't know how much I love you my Sweetheart and . . . I'll not relax until I can hold you tight again.'

CHAPTER ELEVEN

'We've been very happy'

1953–70   *B*y the mid-1950s the Windsors had created a life for themselves in exile which, if not what they would ideally have wished, revolved around a plan of sorts and did not lack comfort and style. They were the owners of two fine properties in France – their town house in the Bois de Boulogne, ideally designed for formal entertaining, and the Moulin de la Tuilerie (known as the Mill), forty minutes' drive away in still relatively unspoilt countryside, where they entertained less formally and had friends to stay. The Duchess was busily engaged in perfecting and running these two houses, organizing their thirty servants and planning their entertainments, while the Duke, when not supporting her in these tasks, was occupied by his English garden at the Mill, his daily round of golf, his business correspondence and his occasional writing projects. After celebrating Christmas at the Mill, they would go to America for three months, basing themselves at the Waldorf in New York and visiting friends at Palm Beach and elsewhere. During August and September they usually enjoyed a summer holiday at some French, Italian or Spanish resort: Biarritz was a favourite haunt in the fifties, Marbella in the late sixties. Visits to England tended to be brief and infrequent, though they sometimes went there in the late autumn, staying at Claridge's, to do some Christmas shopping and see their friends.

Though the Paris house was not especially large, the Duchess (with the assistance of Boudin) contrived to give it a palatial atmosphere as befitted the residence of a former king. The footmen wore the royal livery, and the marbled entrance hall, made to look imposing by the use of *trompe l'oeil*, exhibited the Duke's garter banner and other royal souvenirs. The long blue and silver drawing room was filled with fine eighteenth-century French furniture, full-length portraits of Queen Mary and of the Duke in Garter Robes, and a profusion of exquisite objects. One end of it led to a cosy library, dominated by Brockhurst's striking pre-war portrait of the Duchess, the other to an exotic dining room, its panelling and minstrel galleries obtained from the dismantling of an old château. At night, softly illuminated by innumerable candles and filled with a profusion of orchids (cultivated in the Windsors' own hothouse), it was, as one guest recalled, 'like stepping into a fairyland of fantastic luxury'.

The Mill consisted of several rustic buildings, one of which had been converted into an immense barn of a sitting room filled with souvenirs of the Duke's career, including the table on which the Abdication had been signed and a wall map illustrating his travels as Prince of Wales. The Duke came to love the Mill rather as he had done the Fort, and laboured for several years to create an English garden there with the help of Russell Page, the leading English professional gardener of his generation. Some felt the Mill was his province just as the Paris house was hers: but it was the Duchess who stage-managed the less formal life at the Mill just as she organized their Paris parties. 'The whole atmosphere was intensely unstrained', wrote James Pope-Hennessy after staying there in 1958, 'owing, I should say, to the Duchess and the job she has done on the Duke. . . . Every conceivable luxury and creature-comfort is conscripted to produce a perfection of sybaritic living. It is, of course, intensely   American.
. . . The Queen Mother at Clarence House is leading a lodging-house existence compared to this.'

The impression of opulence created by the Windsors' hospitality was the result not so much of an extravagant mode of living as the Duchess's perfectionism and attention to detail. She worked tirelessly to ensure that all was comfortable and pleasing to the eye. Under her direction, her chef produced meals which were not only lavish and delicious but also original and memorable. She also took care in choosing and training her servants, whom she treated with consideration and many of whom became devoted to her.

The Windsors attracted comment owing to the fact that, whenever they travelled to America or elsewhere, they were accompanied by a small retinue of servants and secretaries and an enormous quantity of luggage, which seemed something of an extravagance in the 1960s. The Duke however had been used to travelling in such a manner in his princely days, and once again the Duchess felt it important that he should enjoy the comforts of his former rank. The numerous travelling trunks contained not just their wardrobe but a collection

The house in the Bois de Boulogne.

of ornamental and sentimental objects, as well as quantities of china, glass and linen, so that the Duke should always feel at home wherever they might be.

Their life was essentially one of entertainment; but this was hardly unusual in the case of a well-to-do aristocratic couple in their sixties, living in retirement abroad, who enjoyed society but were without strong intellectual interests and did not belong to any closely defined set. No doubt they would have enjoyed a different and more fulfilling existence had they been welcomed back to the British royal fold, and the Duke been given a suitable official role; but it was hardly their fault that they were denied these opportunities. As always, the Duchess's guiding principle was that, as the Duke had given up a throne for her, it was her duty to create as royal an existence for them as their circumstances would allow: and at least they were able to entertain royally and be treated as royal guests of honour at the many parties and charity functions they attended in Paris and New York. The endless round of entertainment organized by the Duchess also ensured that idleness and boredom, so fatal to her

The Moulin de la Tuilerie at Gif-sur-Yvette (opposite) and the Duke's garden (above).

husband's morale, were generally kept at bay. 'It is all very merry and very happy', commented Pope-Hennessy; 'life is quite blazingly a romp and must be kept that way. . . .'

Many people wanted to meet the Windsors and they were not difficult to meet; but their intimate circle was fairly distinguished on the whole. The Duke kept up with old friends in England such as Walter Monckton, Lord Dudley, Lord Brownlow and Lord Sefton; they saw much of other upper-class English residents of Paris such as Lord Tennyson, Lady Diana Cooper, the Loel Guinnesses and the Mosleys; and they associated with fellow exiled royals such as Prince Dmitri of Russia, and King Leopold of the Belgians and his morganatic wife Princess de Réthy. They knew members of the French aristocracy and political establishment: De Gaulle's defence minister General Billotte was a friend. The Windsors were stars in their way and enjoyed meeting other stars such as Cole Porter, Marlene Dietrich and Richard Burton; they were said to be prominent in the international set of wealthy celebrities and their hangers-on known as café society, but this mainly applied to the New York side of their lives. Pope-Hennessy felt they were 'too open and trusting towards others': as a stranger, he received a tremendous welcome from them when he went to see the Duke in connection with his biography of Queen Mary, but felt that 'so much enthusiasm might suddenly gell up and one would be in the limbo reserved for the many, many people who have treated them badly or turned out to be a disappointment. . . .'

Although there were many people whose society they enjoyed, some of whom they trusted and had known for a long time, it must be said that the Windsors, like many close couples, tended to be wrapped up in each other and reserve their intense feelings and loyalties for each other. At dinners and parties they could always be seen glancing at or looking for each other, he because he never had eyes for anyone else, she to make sure he was content. ('She noticed in a second if someone was boring him', recalled Diana Mosley of the Duchess as a hostess, 'and moved everyone round.') After Aunt Bessie's death in 1964, neither of them had any relations to whom they felt close. Their spare affection was lavished on their dogs, the pugs Trooper, Disraeli, Ginseng, Davy Crockett and Black Diamond, who were spoiled and pampered (though the Duchess never allowed them to get fat) and whose tastes and moods were a subject of absorbing concern to their owners. They were sociable animals, forever leaning

Above At a ball in New York, 1959, with Mrs Winston Guest and Hervé Alphand,
French Ambassador to the United States.

Below The pug lovers.

The Duke, on a visit to London, emerging from Lock's the hatter in St James's Street.

on and sniffing at the ankles of guests. The Windsors also collected porcelain pugs (mostly Meissen) which they displayed on an occasional table in their Paris house.

Illness and depression took their toll on the Duke in later years, and many found he had lost his sparkle and become rather dull. But all were impressed by his courtesy, and in the right company he could still exhibit much of his old fascination and charm. The Duchess meanwhile retained her liveliness and alertness into her early seventies. Pope-Hennessy thought her less intelligent than her husband, but was struck by her 'stern power of concentration' and 'immense goodwill'. She was a vigilant hostess, missing nothing as she kept her eyes on her husband, guests and staff.

They both continued to dress stylishly and be of intense interest to the fashion world. The Duke wore beautiful clothes in an individual way, and was not afraid to experiment with the most garish American fabrics. The Duchess was always regarded as one of the best dressed women in the world, and treasured by her couturiers Balenciaga and Givenchy. They both took care to remain elegantly thin. While the Duke, having retained youthful looks up to his fifties, aged rapidly thereafter, the Duchess did not disdain to defy the ageing process with face-lifts and other treatments: in conjunction with her taste for trying out the latest crazes, such as the mini skirt and the twist, this gave her a rather odd look, though declaring to the world her undiminished zest for life.

It has been said that the Windsors were extremely rich. In fact they were only moderately rich, but they nevertheless succeeded in living the life of the very rich and keeping up a royal style. This was achieved thanks to the tax privileges they enjoyed in France, the Duchess's housekeeping talents, and the fact that, in appropriate cases (such as that of hotels which obviously benefited from having such famous guests), they took advantage of their celebrity to secure preferential terms. It is not true that they accepted 'attendance money' to appear at functions, or were late in paying their bills: the Duke was in fact punctilious in such matters. It is true that they were sometimes entertained by and received presents from wealthy tycoons who were not perhaps distinguished in other ways, but it would be wrong to suggest that they associated with such people purely in the hope of advantage, for the Duke was genuinely fascinated by successful businessmen and intrgued as to how they had made their money.

Below The Duchess, dressed in black velvet and arm-in-arm with Pamela Harriman, leaves the memorial service in Paris for Christian Dior, 1957.

Above With the American society columnist Elsa Maxwell.

Below With John F. Kennedy at a New York dinner.

The only opportunity they had to earn money themselves was to write books and articles with editorial assistance, and the sums thus raised made a vital contribution to their circumstances. The Duke's memoirs, published in 1951, enabled them to buy and restore the Mill; and the Duchess began work on her autobiography two years later when they were faced with the expense of moving into their Paris house. Published in 1956 under the title *The Heart Has Its Reasons*, it shows an extraordinary memory for detail, and its style is not as uncharacteristic as has been supposed. She was candid about many aspects of her early life, and as honest about the development of her relationship with the Duke as she could have been without hurting him, making clear that she had tried to escape from him and so keep him on his throne. The book was a success with the public and fascinating to psychiatrists, who recommended it to patients who were disturbed as a result of receiving passionate attentions which they found it difficult to respond to or understand.

During the autumn of 1955 the Duchess went to New York for two months to finish writing her book, persuading the Duke (whose company would have been a distraction) to stay behind to work on his garden at the Mill. This was the last time they were parted during their marriage and hence the last occasion on which they exchanged long letters. These confirm that the essence of their relationship had hardly changed during the previous twenty years. The Duke writes of how dreadfully he misses her and feels lost without her. Her replies are both protective and admonishing: she begs him not to sleep in a certain bedroom owing to the fire risk, but warns him to be considerate to the staff as 'if the servants leave I will too!' The letters are also interesting in that they show the Duke's reactions to the Margaret-Townsend affair, which reached its tragic end at this time. 'The unctuous hypocritical cant and corn . . . has been hard to take. The Church of England has won again but this time they caught their fly while I was lucky enough to escape. . . .'

In the early 1960s the Duke accepted a financially generous offer from the producer Jack le Vien to make a film version of his memoirs. This was largely based on old newsreels and created a slightly odd impression, the narration by Orson Welles in his deep American voice being interspersed with footage of the Duke, looking nervous and unwell, sitting with the Duchess in the garden at the Mill and reciting passages from his book which he had imperfectly learnt by heart. It did however make the point that he had abdicated out of honourable motives and thereby secured domestic happiness, while saying nothing to which the Royal Family might reasonably object. At the première in Paris the Duke was seen to be in tears. As he got up to leave, Gore Vidal thought he heard him tell the Duchess that he would have done it all again, to which she replied: 'I wouldn't!'

The 1960s saw a slight thaw in the Duke's relations with his family. There were few cordial meetings, but he received royal permission to do various things that would have been unthinkable under George VI. In 1949, for example, when he had been writing his memoirs, a request to allow his researcher to use the Royal Archives had met with a blank refusal; but when he was engaged on another small book of reminiscences a decade later, his assistant, Lord Kinross, was given the necessary permission. After it had become known, to widespread dismay in Great Britain, that the Windsors had purchased a burial plot in Baltimore, the Queen agreed to their being buried together in a private

At the Mill during the filming of *A King's Story*.

At a Paris costume ball on the eve of the Duke's seventieth birthday, 1964 (left).
Walking in a London park after the Duke's eye operation, 1965 (right).

mausoleum in the grounds of Frogmore, his boyhood home on the Windsor estate; and when, a few years later, he asked if they might in fact be buried not in a mausoleum but in the Royal Family's own burial ground nearby, she assented to this also. In 1964, when he underwent open heart surgery in Texas, the Queen sent him flowers; and when a few months later he underwent an eye operation at a London clinic, she sent him a hamper of wine and *foie gras* and eventually called to see him personally, thus meeting the Duchess for the first time since 1936. He asked if he might walk in the gardens of Buckingham Palace during his convalescence, and the Queen agreed to his doing so, accompanied not by the Duchess but his valet: since the Queen Mother still harboured rancorous feelings towards the Duchess, there were limits to the royal indulgence.

The most significant act of reconciliation took place in June 1967, a few days after the Windsors' thirtieth wedding anniversary, when they accepted an invitation from the Queen to attend the unveiling of a memorial to Queen Mary at Marlborough House, her former London residence, most of the Royal Family being present. The ceremony, originally due to take place on Queen Mary's

More than thirty years after the Abdication, the Duchess formally meets the Queen and other members of the Royal Family at a ceremony in London in memory of Queen Mary, 7 June 1967.

centenary at the end of May, was in fact delayed for two weeks to enable the Windsors to attend. The Duchess curtsied to the Queen but failed to do so to the Queen Mother, with whom however she appeared to chat amiably for some moments. Observing the photographs of the occasion, Diana Mosley thought that 'the Duchess in her Paris clothes looked like a denizen of another planet, among the flowery toques and the pastel overcoats'. The ceremony lasted exactly fifteen minutes – thus satisfying the Duke's wartime plea for a 'once only meeting of a quarter of an hour' in order to put an end to the assumption that his family regarded his wife as an outcast.

In January 1970 the Windsors appeared on British television together when they were interviewed by Kenneth Harris, the programme attracting an audience of almost twelve million. They appeared charming and relaxed, and the tender looks they exchanged, and their easy badinage, gave the impression that they were close and happy in old age. They gave no hint of bitterness. Asked if she had any regrets, the Duchess replied that she wished some things could have been different but that, like everyone else, they had had to take the rough with the smooth. Asked if he might have served his country after the Abdication, the Duke exchanged a meaningful glance with his wife but drew himself up with a sudden: 'Hard to say!' Mostly however they talked of their domestic life, and their delight in each other was evident. At one point, as she spoke of her failure to cure him of his lifelong unpunctuality, they suddenly joined hands. It is said that the camera cannot lie. 'We've been very happy', she said; and few who watched them could doubt it.

The grief-stricken Duchess appears at a window of Buckingham Palace, 3 June 1972.

CHAPTER TWELVE

'He gave up so much for me'

1970–86   The Windsors were getting old. In the year following their successful television appearance, their health sharply declined. The Duke suffered from a multitude of ailments, and they decided to sell the Mill as he was no longer fit enough to work in the garden. The Duchess, hitherto known for her alertness, would sometimes lose the thread of conversation or forget orders she had given servants – probably on account of arteriosclerosis which interfered with the blood supply to her brain. A liver complaint affected her nerves, and this in turn provoked her old stomach trouble. Cecil Beaton, who visited the Windsors in September 1970, found that she had 'suddenly aged' and 'become a little old woman'; though as energetic and trim as ever, she 'had the sad, haunted eyes of the ill'. The Duke seemed a physical wreck, but still displayed flashes of his old charm and was clearly as happy as ever with his wife. 'These two old people, very bent, but full of spirit and still dandies, stood at the door as I went off. . . .'

A third of a century had passed since the Abdication and they were now sought-after celebrities. In 1970, on their last visit to America together, President Nixon and his wife gave a great party for them at the White House, to which many of the Duchess's relations and old friends were asked. In October 1971 Emperor Hirohito called to see them in Paris on his European tour, the two men reminiscing about their previous meeting in Japan in 1922. That same month Prince Charles made an impromptu visit to his great-uncle late one evening, astounding the Windsors' dinner guests. He recorded an affectionate talk with the Duke, who did however mention 'how difficult the family had made it for him these past 33 years. . . .' Meanwhile the Duchess 'kept flitting to and fro like a strange bat', striking the Prince as 'unsympathetic and somewhat superficial . . . that brilliant hostess type charm but without feeling. . . .'

Six weeks later, the Duke, who had been a heavy smoker all his adult life and whose voice had diminished to a hoarse whisper, was diagnosed as suffering from cancer of the larynx, too advanced for an operation to be possible. A painful course of cobalt treatment brought little respite, but for a while he nevertheless insisted on going out as usual with his wife and entertaining at home, his main concern being that she should not see how ill he was. By the end of March 1972 he was emaciated and bedridden and being cared for by nurses: the Duchess was beside herself with anxiety but affected to carry on as normal, as he wished.

The Queen was due to make a state visit to Paris that spring and decided to call on her uncle, about whose medical condition she knew more than the Duchess. This she did on 18 May, accompanied by her husband and Prince Charles. The visit involved much preparation as the Duke insisted on seeing the Queen not in his bedroom but fully dressed in the adjoining sitting room,

With Richard Nixon, September 1970.

with the life-sustaining apparatus to which he was now attached concealed behind a curtain. The Duchess received the royal party and gave them tea, the conversation never touching on the subject that filled all their minds. Then the Queen went upstairs to see to the Duke, who struggled to his feet and bowed. (The doctor, who had not foreseen this move, was 'terrified that the apparatus would come apart before our eyes. Fortunately it held in place, and I don't think anything was noticed.') They talked in private for ten minutes. The Duchess was photographed curtsying deeply to the Queen as she departed.

The Duke died at two o'clock on the morning of Sunday 28 May 1972. There is some dispute as to his last words: according to his Irish nurse, they were 'England – the waste!', while his Bahamian valet Sidney Johnson recalled them to have been 'Mama! Mama!', which he took to be a cry for the Duchess. The Duchess was immediately summoned: she took his hand with the words 'my David', kissed his forehead, and stood there silently – her silence being

The Duchess drops a low curtsey to the Queen, who has just visited her dying uncle, 18 May 1972.

more poignant than tears, which were shed for her by the others present. She displayed courage during the next twenty-four hours, and was able to cope with the many practical arrangements, as well as receiving the King of Italy and French Foreign Minister who came to pay their respects, and Hubert de Givenchy who fitted her for her mourning clothes; but then she seems to have suffered a collapse, the result of the accumulated strain of recent months and a sudden dawning of the enormity of her loss. She nevertheless flew to England on 2 June to participate in the funeral ceremonies, accompanied by her American doctor, her French maid, and Grace Dudley, the widow of one of the Duke's oldest friends.

At Heathrow airport she was met by Lord Mountbatten, who drove her to Buckingham Palace where she was to spend three nights in the suite normally reserved for visiting heads of state. She dined with the Royal Family that evening: Prince Charles noted that she 'prattled away throughout the meal', and wondered whether this was a 'brilliant façade' to hide the strain 'or whether she was really like this all the time and didn't really notice Uncle David's departure'. The next day (which would have been their thirty-fifth wedding anniversary) she watched on television the Queen's Birthday Parade, during which the pipers of the Scots and Welsh Guards played the lament *The Flowers of the Forest* in the Duke's memory. That evening, accompanied by Mountbatten and Prince Charles, she attended the Duke's lying-in-state at Windsor after it had been closed to the public, some sixty thousand of whom had come to pay their respects to him over the past two days. She 'stood alone, a frail, tiny black figure, gazing at the coffin and bowing briefly. . . .' Finally, in 'the saddest imaginable voice', she said: 'He was my entire life. I can't begin to think what I am going to do without him, he gave up so much for me, and now he is gone. I always hoped I would die before him.'

The brief but moving funeral service took place two days later at St George's Chapel, the Duchess sitting with the Queen. Afterwards there was a luncheon at the castle, at which the Duchess was placed between Mountbatten and Prince Philip. She later told friends that the two Battenbergs, their mouths full of rice pudding, had asked her quite blatantly what she meant to do with the Duke's archives and other possessions, and whether she proposed to return to spend her last years in America. To this last question she replied: 'Don't worry, I shan't be coming back here, if that's what you're thinking.'

After lunch the Duke's coffin was interred at the royal burial ground at Frogmore, beneath the shade of a great plane tree. (The Duchess noticed that the space reserved for herself seemed exceedingly small, and subsequently remarked on this, as a result of which a hedge was moved to make more room for her.) That afternoon, as the Duchess returned to Paris, the Commons and Lords debated a resolution expressing their sympathy to the Royal Family following the death of the ex-King. Two Members of Parliament, the Protestant Unionist Ian Paisley and the Liberal Leader Jeremy Thorpe (whose parents had known Mrs Simpson in the middle class London world of the 1930s), expressed dismay that the Duchess had not been mentioned in the resolution, which was duly amended to include her: Thorpe spoke of the Duke's love for her, and of her 'composure and dignity' which had 'won our deep respect'.

The Duchess continued to enjoy three-and-a-half years of relatively normal existence; but with the death of the Duke, whom she had devoted the past thirty-five years to looking after and keeping happy, the purpose had gone out of her life. She continued to live in their Paris house. Like Queen Victoria, she kept her husband's things exactly as he had left them, down to the clothes in their cupboards and the cigars in their boxes, and every evening would go to his room, still adorned with numerous pictures of herself, and whisper: 'Good night, David.' She still had valued and devoted friends, though there was a greater number who sought her company but whom she did not particularly want to see. She went to Biarritz in August 1972 with her old friend Foxy Sefton, and during the autumn started going out and entertaining again on a small scale. She continued to take care over her appearance. An unusually sympathetic British ambassadorial couple, Sir Edward and Lady Tomkins, showed her greater kindness than any of their predecessors, and gave a number of dinners in her honour, though still unable to treat her as royalty. She ate less but drank more, as a result of which her ulcer flared up from time to time. Shortly before Christmas 1972 she suffered a bad fall and broke her hip, the first of several such accidents. In the summer of 1973 she visited the South of France and also made a day trip to England to see the Duke's gravestone, at which she was photographed with Mountbatten and the Duke of Kent.

She visited New York again during the spring of 1974, sailing from Cannes on the Italian liner *Rafaello* and staying at an apartment at the Waldorf put at her disposal by her friend Nathaniel Cummings, President of Consolidated

Above The Duke's coffin borne into St George's Chapel by a party of Welsh Guardsmen, 5 June 1972.

Left & opposite The Duchess leaves the funeral service, accompanied by the Queen and followed by Prince Philip, the Queen Mother and King Olaf of Norway.

The Duchess at the Duke's grave in July 1973, with Lord Mountbatten and the Duke of Kent.

Foods Inc. The many friends she saw there admired her courage and energy in view of her evident frailty. She also retained something of her old elegance, turning heads as she emerged from the hotel lift. Sometimes she behaved irrationally, as when, dining with Gore Vidal, she tried out some distantly remembered Chinese words on a Puerto Rican waiter. But on the whole she seemed quite lucid and well. Princess Margaret and Lord Snowdon called on her during her visit, as they happened to be staying at the same hotel, and they were photographed together.

By a will made shortly before his death, the Duke had bequeathed his entire estate to the Duchess, on the understanding that she, when her turn came, would remember friends, servants and charities. (Had she predeceased him, the will named a list of English, French and American charities as joint beneficia-

With Princess Margaret and Lord Snowdon in New York, May 1974.

ries.) The Duchess was reputed to be a very rich widow but (except in the sense that she owned jewellery and other possessions which, after her death, would turn out to be immensely valuable) this was not really the case. The Windsors had lived beyond their means in recent years and their fortune was much diminished. Even after the Mill had been sold with most of its contents, and it had been confirmed (after long negotiations) that the Duchess would not be required by the French Government to pay either estate duty or income tax, she found herself having to cut down her staff from about thirty to a dozen and generally curb her expenditure.

While discovering these unwelcome truths about her circumstances, the Duchess was being approached by a multitude of people requesting souvenirs of the Duke or suggesting what she should do with her money. The most insistent of these was Lord Mountbatten, whom the Duke had warned her not to trust. On the first of several visits to the widowed Duchess in Paris, Mountbatten asked to be given some valuable objects which he claimed the Duke had intended him to have. She agreed to his suggestion that the Duke's uniforms and decorations be returned to England, but was embarrassed by his heavy-handed requests that she devote her fortune to setting up a foundation under his control. The Duchess also felt vulnerable owing to her dependence on her private secretary John Utter, a former American diplomat with whom the Duke had quarrelled towards the end of his life.

In these circumstances the Duchess turned to Maître Suzanne Blum, a formidable Frenchwoman, only two years younger than herself, who had been her French lawyer for the past twenty years. Maître Blum had made an outstanding career and been close to many of the leading French literary and political figures of her time. Her instincts were intensely protective and she felt the Duchess deserved much support after the treatment she had received from the British Establishment and the world's press. It was Maître Blum who had negotiated the Duchess's favourable tax treatment with the French authorities, and she never failed to register a vigorous protest whenever the Duchess's privacy was violated or her reputation maligned. Early in 1973 the Duchess gave Maître Blum a general power over her affairs (except for her finances which were entrusted to another professional), and during the next two years she sent a stream of handwritten notes to her lawyer expressing her affection and gratitude. The Duchess insisted that Maître Blum should always be present during

Lord Mountbatten's visits as she had the necessary strength of personality to stand up to that forceful character.

In February 1975 the Duchess, who had been upset by Frances Donaldson's recent biography of the Duke, was surprised to discover that the bulk of her and the Duke's papers had been transferred to the Royal Archives at Windsor without her knowledge (though with the connivance of her secretary Utter who left her service around this time). She promptly gave her remaining papers to Maître Blum along with a power enabling her to authorize their eventual publication. Around this time also, the Duchess made a will appointing as her principal legatee the Pasteur Institute, the great international medical foundation based in France. It had always been her intention to express in some such way her gratitude to France for all the kindness and privilege she and the Duke had enjoyed there, and she had already, two years earlier, arranged for the best of her furniture and porcelain to go in due course to French museums.

On 13 November 1975 the Duchess suffered a massive intestinal haemorrhage, following which she lay close to death at the American Hospital for some weeks. Eventually she recovered, though with her physical and mental powers severely impaired, and she returned home in the early spring of 1976, never to leave again except for further hospital visits. Amazingly, she lived on for another ten years, devotedly cared for by her butler Georges, his wife Ofélia and her doctor Jean Thin. During the remainder of the 1970s she still received a few intimate friends, and was able to enjoy her garden occasionally. In 1980 however she lost the power of speech and henceforth access to her was virtually confined to her staff, her nurses, Dr Thin and Maître Blum. There was no point in her seeing friends with whom she could not communicate, and it would have caused her added distress to be seen in her pitiable state. It was Maître Blum's task to keep the world at bay, and bizarre rumours developed that her client was being 'kept alive' for some purpose. In fact, the Duchess was never 'kept alive' except in that she received the best nursing attention and was cured of ailments and infections in a routine way; nor did anyone have an interest in prolonging her sad existence, least of all Maître Blum, who feared she would not herself survive to fulfil her designated role as the Duchess's executor, and who went blind during these years.

In the autumn of 1979 Maître Blum, who had been upset by the portrayal of the Duchess in a recent television series, asked me to write a number of books

In her Paris garden,
September 1974.

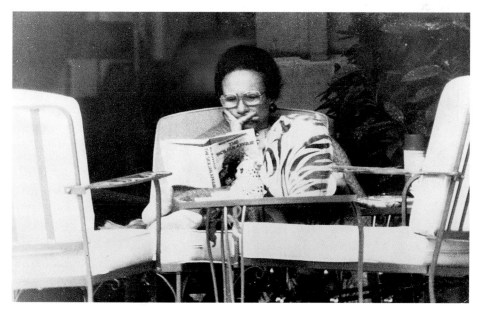

based on the Windsors' papers and putting forward their point of view. When I joined her in Paris in February 1980 to begin work on the papers, she told me that the Duchess might die at any moment and was not expected to survive the year. The Maître was an extraordinary personality, who throughout her long career had taken the causes of her clients to heart, and she felt strongly that the Windsors had been mistreated and maligned and that it was her duty to protect their interests and reputation staunchly. She was a chivalrous woman of great ability and it was easy to understand why the Duchess so valued her.

Every Saturday Maître Blum would visit the Duchess's house, where she had long talks with Georges the butler about his mistress's current condition and any matters requiring attention, and I sometimes accompanied her on these visits. The house had a faded, sepulchral grandeur, the décor becoming slightly shabby and the lights turned low to save electricity. The main sounds were those of the two ancient surviving pugs as they yapped shrilly, wheezed asthmatically and clattered along the floors. I only once saw the Duchess for a few moments, when I went up to her room with Georges and Maître Blum in the autumn of 1980. One noticed her brilliant, blinking blue eyes, her high cheekbones, and her square hands in constant agitated movement above the counterpane. Her hair was white and wispy, her mouth a gash, her skin smooth. Although she could not communicate, she seemed to recognize her butler and lawyer and one felt she was still faintly in touch with the world.

The Duchess of Windsor died on 24 April 1986, a few weeks short of her ninetieth birthday. Her remains were flown to England and, following a funeral service at St George's Chapel which was remarkable in that her name was not once mentioned from beginning to end, she was interred next to her husband in the burial ground at Frogmore.

Opposite above Maître Suzanne Blum in 1982.

Opposite below The Duchess with her pugs, shortly before her collapse in November 1975.

Overleaf The Duchess's coffin arrives at RAF Benson on its final journey to Windsor, 27 April 1986.

Epilogue

It has been claimed that, to the end of her long and often adventurous life, the Duchess of Windsor remained a virgin. This apparently astonishing view came to my knowledge during the 1980s from two independent and convincing sources – Maître Suzanne Blum, her long-standing Paris lawyer, and Dr John Randell, an eminent consultant at Charing Cross Hospital in London who specialised in the borderline between men and women. Later, I learned from another well-informed source of the Duchess's reported remarks to Herman Rogers, that she had never suffered to be touched 'below the Mason-Dixon Line' or consummated her first two marriages. There can be no harm in mentioning such matters now she has been dead for ten years and left no-one behind her. The element of virginity would explain much of her other-worldliness, and add to an understanding of her relationship with the man who gave up a throne for her. It would enable one to appreciate the literal truth of Walter Monckton's statement that it would be 'a great mistake to assume that he [King Edward] was merely in love with her in the ordinary physical sense of the term', and of Winston Churchill's suggestion that the affair 'was psychical rather than sexual, and certainly not sensual except incidentally'.

Strange though the comparison may seem, spanning as it does almost four centuries, the Duchess had much in common with Queen Elizabeth I, her first cousin by marriage twelve times removed. Both women underwent early experiences which toughened their characters; both were great wearers of clothes and jewellery, loved making merry, and were obsessed by housekeeping; both were flirtatious, and enjoyed the company of men; and both are alleged to have been virgins. In both cases, their alleged virginity was said to have been rooted in an incapacity for sexual intercourse and childbearing, though both also seem to have suffered a trauma in childhood which affected their attitude to sex. The playwright Ben Jonson believed the Queen 'had a membrana on her, which made her incapable of man, though for her delight she tryed many'. In *Elizabeth and Essex*, Lytton Strachey wrote: 'Though the precious citidel was

never to be violated, there were outworks and bastions over which exciting bat-
tles might be fought, and which might even, at moments, be allowed to fall into
the bold hands of an assailant.'

In her famous speech at Tilbury, Elizabeth claimed to posssess 'the heart and
stomach of a man'; and Wallis, for all her feminine wiles and mastery of feminine arts, exhibited an abundance of masculine characteristics. One who knew
her well has described her as having 'a man's brain', a reference to her capacity
for dominating and organising. In outward physical terms, her hair was thick
and straight, her jaw was large and square, and she was flat-chested. One of the
reasons she kept herself so thin is that, when she put on weight, she tended to
develop a wrestler-like physique, striking Cecil Beaton as 'raw-boned and
brawny' at their first meeting in 1935. Her voice was a full-throated contralto.
James Pope-Hennessy found her 'phenomenal' to look at, so 'flat and angular'
that she 'could have been designed for a medieval playing card'; he would have
been 'tempted to classify her as An American Woman _par excellence_, were it not
for the suspicion that she is not a woman at all'.

In her memoirs, the Duchess wrote that hers was the story 'of an ordinary
life that became extraordinary', and went on to write candidly about her short-
comings. She had never been beautiful or pretty; no-one could accuse her of
being an intellectual; she had no ear for music, no mathematical ability; she had
tended to avoid hard decisions in life and seek the easy way out. One might go
further, and say she was a woman who, though possessing strong principles,
lived largely on the surface, without much of an inner life; that she was an
indoor woman who was not much alive to the beauties of nature (except for
flowers, which she treated as an instrument of interior decoration); that she saw
the world too much in terms of her own preoccupations; that she was sometimes seriously imperceptive; and that she lacked a sense of artistic apprecia-
tion, unless one includes the arts of housekeeping, decoration and fashion.

But of those arts, what a mistress she was! By any standards, she must be
judged one of the great domestic organisers of her time. She could transform a
derelict mill into 'a perfection of sybaritic living', or make a huge and ugly villa
look 'as if a family of cheerful good taste had lived there for centuries'. She was
an unrelenting perfectionist in all she undertook. She was quick to learn, and
amazingly adaptable: five years after running a small flat in London, she was
hiring magnificent properties and huge staffs as if she had been used to such

things all her life. With her natural elegance, her keen original taste in clothes and jewellery, her knowledge of how to create an effect, she was a work of art in herself. She was a life enhancer, quick-witted and extrovert, full of enthusiasm and goodwill, able to create an atmosphere of enjoyment around her and make a party go. Gore Vidal, who knew her in her sixties, admired her 'flapper's wisecracking charm'; and even Prince Charles, who met her when she was elderly and ailing and did not care for her, acknowledged her 'brilliant hostess type charm'. A young officer who was assigned to look after her in Bermuda in 1940 found that she possessed 'to an infinite degree that really great gift for making you feel that you are the very person whom she has been waiting all her life to meet'.

She believed that her descent from two contrasting families, the stern Warfields and fey Montagues, had suffused her character with paradox and ambiguity; and a study of her life would seem to bear this out. She was a mixture of the feminine and the masculine; by turns, her behaviour appears wise and rash, conventional and adventurous, considerate and thoughtless, serious and light-hearted, calculating and spontaneous. She was timorous, afraid of thunderstorms and aeroplanes, yet capable of great courage. She has been portrayed as a hedonist, whose main thought in life was to enjoy herself; but no-one worked harder at giving enjoyment to others.

In middle life, she experienced the ultimate fairy tale, becoming the adored favourite of the most glamorous bachelor of his time. The idyll went wrong when, ignoring her pleas, he threw up his position to spend the rest of his life with her. It represented for him both a sacrifice and a liberation, for her a stupendous acquisition of resposibilities she never desired or sought, coming in circumstances which brought upon her the world's hostility. She faced up to all bravely, and proceeded to devote the rest of her life to the man who loved her, who for his part, despite the heartache of ostracism and exile, never ceased to feel that the realisation of his happiness had been worth a throne.

Select bibliography

Cecil Beaton, *The Wandering Years* (1961)
────── *The Parting Years* (1978)

Lord Birkenhead, *Walter Monckton* (1969)

Michael Bloch, *The Duke of Windsor's War* (1982)
────── *Operation Willi* (1984)
────── *Wallis & Edward: The Intimate Correspondence of the Duke and Duchess of Windsor* (1986)
────── *The Secret File of the Duke of Windsor* (1988)
────── *The Reign & Abdication of Edward VIII* (1990)

Sarah Bradford, *Elizabeth: A Biography of Her Majesty* (1996)

J. Bryan III and Charles J.V. Murphy, *The Windsor Story* (1979)

Jonathan Dimbleby, *The Prince of Wales* (1994)

Frances Donaldson, *Edward VIII* (1974)

Martin Gilbert, *Winston S. Churchill 1922–1939* (1976)

Dina Welles Hood, *Working for the Windsors* (1957)

Robert Rhodes James (ed.), *Chips: The Diaries of Sir Henry Channon* (1969)

Susan Lowndes (ed.), *Diaries and Letters of Marie Belloc Lowndes, 1911–1947* (1971)

Suzy Menkes, *The Windsor Style* (1987)

Diana Mosley, *The Duchess of Windsor* (1980)

Harold Nicolson, *Diaries and Letters* (1966–68)

James Pope-Hennessy, *Queen Mary* (1959)

Peter Quennell, *A Lonely Business: A Self-Portrait of James Pope-Hennessy* (1981)

Andrew Roberts, *Eminent Churchillians* (1994)

Kenneth Rose, *King George V* (1983)

Donald Spoto, *Dynasty* (1995)

Lytton Strachey, *Elizabeth and Essex* (1928)

Michael Thornton, *Royal Feud* (1985)

Gore Vidal, *Palimpsest* (1995)

Sir John Wheeler-Bennett, *The Life and Reign of King George VI* (1958)

Duchess of Windsor, *The Heart has its Reasons* (1956)

Duke of Windsor, *A King's Story* (1951)
——— *The Crown and the People* (1953)
——— *A Family Album* (1960)

Philip Ziegler, *Mountbatten* (1985)
——— *King Edward VIII* (1990)

Index

PHOTOGRAPHIC ACKNOWLEDGEMENTS

Illustrations are from the author's collection, with the exception of the following: letters of the Duke and Duchess of Windsor (pages 36, 43, 45–6, 52, 60, 62, 68, 74, 86, 103, 112–13, 115), reproduced by kind permission of Curtis Brown Ltd; items from sale catalogue of *The Jewels of the Duchess of Windsor*, Sotheby's Geneva, April 1987 (pages 54–5, 80, 87, 94, 119, 152), reproduced by kind permission of Sotheby's plc; and the photographs on pages 12, 30, 32 (bottom), 34, 35 (bottom), 51, 62, 68, 73, 134 (bottom), 137, 138 (top), 180, 183, 185, 188–9, 199–201, 203–4, 206, 208, 209 (left), 210, 212, 214, 215, 218, 219 (top), 220, 223, 226–7, reproduced by kind permission of Associated Newspapers Limited.

Credit is due to the following in respect of illustrations on the indicated pages: Bertram Park (24, 40, 68, 70); Sir William Rothenstein (35, bottom left); Dorothy Wilding (48, 203); Henry Cecil (58); Betty Hanley (118); Etienne Drian (124); O. Gremela (140); Mary Espírito Santo Salgado (155); Stanley Toogood (158, 160–1, 163, 166–7); Gerald Brockhurst (166, top); Baron (180); Nick de Morgoli (206, bottom); Elizabeth Johnson (219, bottom): Daniel Angeli (223); Dmitri Kasterine (224, top); Mike Forster (226–7).

The author and publishers would welcome information enabling them to rectify any inadvertent omission of acknowledgement or credit in future impressions of this work.

own spoon. which I
borrowed from Osborne
for the marking.
Your obedient servant
Wallis

Friday, June 28th

Ambassador 2215

5. Bryanston Court,
Bryanston Square,
W.1.

Sir —

Many Happy Returns
of the day. This small
"presy" is to conceal
Bryant & May's Forks
on your dining table
+ the Fort. I am
enclosing your

H.R.H. The Prince of Wales K.G.

Memorandum
To
Wallis
Good morning
my sweetheart
Thank God

after lovely
Your lovely
year

King it's only a
matter of how long
and I won't be
able to put up

Good night
Why do I
hard things
on the
sometimes
things
prefer for a few minutes
if he's worst —
But I do long long
to see you even

SANDRINGHAM, NORFOLK.

My own Sweetheart
Just a line to
say I love you more
and more and need
you so to be with me
at this difficult time
There is no hope
whatsoever for the

Sat y